RODNEY PLUNKE

D1085861

BASIC INTRODUCTION TO
THE NEW TESTAMENT

Basic Introduction to the New Testament

BY

JOHN R. W. STOTT

author of *Basic Christianity*

WM. B. EERDMANS PUBLISHING CO.

GRAND RAPIDS, MICHIGAN

First American Edition, 1964, published by arrangement
with Longmans, Green and Co. Ltd., London. Originally
published 1954 as *Men with a message*.

ISBN 0-8028-1190-6

First printing, June 1964
Second printing, December 1964
Third printing, November 1966
Fourth printing, February 1968
Fifth printing, April 1970
Sixth printing, November 1972

PHOTOLITHOPRINTED BY GRAND RAPIDS BOOK MANUFACTURERS, INC.
GRAND RAPIDS, MICHIGAN
PRINTED IN THE UNITED STATES OF AMERICA

CONTENTS

INTRODUCTION

Basic Introduction to the New Testament is an attempt to introduce the New Testament, its authors and their writings, to the man in the pew. The practice of daily Bible reading, whether by individual Christians or in family prayers, is becoming rare.

The purpose of this book is to encourage Christian people to read the New Testament for themselves. It is intended to be an incentive to Bible reading, and not a substitute for it. In writing it, I have had two particular themes in mind.

Firstly, I have sought to expound the distinctive contribution of each New Testament author. Many readers find it difficult to see the wood for the trees. The New Testament is the second part of a library. Several different writers have had a share in its composition, and they reflect different points of view. The library is too big in size and too broad in content to grasp easily. It should therefore be a help before reading a passage in the Bible to have a clear understanding of the author's principal message. This method is exposed to the great dangers of over-simplification, omissions and unbalanced emphasis. To give one chapter to Paul's thirteen epistles and one to James's five chapters is to court difficulty, and to include the message of Jesus among the messages of His apostles may seem an irreverence. But these criticisms I am content to face, because it is the teaching of the New Testament as a whole which I hope to summarize, according to the distinctive message of each contributor.

Secondly, I have endeavoured, in the case of the apostolic writers, to introduce the men as well as to expound the message. It is true that what they wrote was determined partly by their knowledge of the gospel tradition, and partly by the needs of the church or individual for whom they were writing. But they were also inspired men. Our Lord had promised that the Spirit of truth would guide them into all the truth (Jn. 16: 12–13). St. Paul claimed that he was proclaiming wisdom which God had revealed through His Spirit and, moreover, that he was imparting it 'in words not taught by human wisdom but taught by the Spirit' (1 Cor. 2: 6–13). In the Second Epistle of Peter, Paul's letters are even ranked with the Scriptures of the Old Testament (2 Pet. 3: 15–16). Nevertheless, they were still men. They were not machines. Their possession by the Holy Spirit did not obliterate their human characteristics. The Holy Spirit first prepared, and then used, their individuality of upbringing, experience, temperament and personality, in order to convey through each some distinctive and appropriate truth. That Paul should have been the apostle of grace and faith, Peter the apostle of hope and John the apostle of love was not an insignificant accident. Each was fitted to be the vehicle of special, divine revelation, and the Holy Spirit Who is the ultimate author, has thus fashioned in the New Testament a jewel which is many-coloured but one.

It is hoped that this introduction to the New Testament will stimulate readers to turn with fresh zeal to the sacred text itself. Large numbers of references have been included, in the further hope that the book may form a basis for more solid Bible study. In order to facilitate this, they have been printed in the text and not relegated to footnotes. The quotations are mostly from the Revised Standard Version. There is no greater need among Christian people in our generation than that we should allow our minds to be conditioned, and our lives reformed, by the Word of God.

Chapter I

THE MESSAGE OF JESUS

The time is fulfilled, and the Kingdom of God is at hand; repent, and believe in the gospel.—Mark 1: 15

WHEN Jesus emerged from the obscurity of His early life in Nazareth and, after His baptism and temptation, began His public ministry, His first recorded words were: 'The time is fulfilled, and the Kingdom of God is at hand; repent, and believe in the gospel' (Mk. 1: 15). The words stand as a concise summary of His message throughout the Galilean ministry, and indeed, when later interpreted by the necessity of His sufferings, of His teaching as a whole. To crowds of simple peasants in Galilee as well as to groups of critical scribes and pharisees His message concerned the character and the coming of the Kingdom of God. He spoke of His Kingdom to Nicodemus by night at the beginning of His ministry (Jn. 3: 1–15), and to Pontius Pilate as the end drew near, in the praetorium at Jerusalem (Jn. 18: 33–8). By pithy proverb and teasing parable, through His words and His works, to the multitudes and the disciples, His dominant theme concerned the Kingdom, what it was, how to enter it and how to live worthily as its citizen. 'I must preach the good news of the Kingdom of God to the other cities also; for I was sent for this purpose' (Lk. 4: 43). 'Soon afterward He went on through cities and villages, preaching and bringing the good news of the Kingdom of God' (Lk. 8: 1).

His first announcement of the good news of the Kingdom (Mk. 1: 15) was introduced by the statement: 'The time is fulfilled.' These words remind us that His theme was not new. He was claiming that the expectation of centuries was now to be fulfilled. The time of which kings had dreamed and seers had prophesied through years of Old Testament history had at last come. Before, therefore, we can understand the teaching of Jesus, especially regarding the character of the Kingdom, it is necessary to look briefly at the Old Testament background.

The Old Testament writers never question the ultimate sovereignty of God. He is supreme in heaven, 'a great King above all gods' (Ps. 95: 3). He is supreme in nature. 'The Lord sat as King at the flood. The Lord sitteth as King for ever' (Ps. 29: 10). He is also supreme in the kingdom of men. 'The Most High rules the kingdom of men' (Dan. 4: 17, 25, 32; 5: 21).

Jeremiah calls Him 'King of the nations' (10: 7). Throughout the varied career of Israel and Judah, exposed to successive waves of tribal invasion and buffeted by the mighty empires of Egypt, Assyria, Babylon, Persia, Greece and Rome, we hear the splendid shout of faith: 'The Lord reigneth' (Ex. 20: 18; 1 Chron. 16: 31; Ps. 93: 1; 96: 10; 97: 1; 99: 1; Is. 52: 7). But the Lord is above all King of Israel. He rescued His people from slavery in Egypt, entered into a solemn covenant with them at Sinai, and during the wilderness wanderings ruled over them as their King. When they entered the promised land, He continued to govern them, and raised up 'judges' like Deborah, Samson, Gideon, and finally Samuel, both to deliver them from marauding tribes and to settle their disputes. But they grew tired of this arrangement, and coming to Samuel, demanded an earthly king 'like all the nations' (1 Sam. 8: 4–9 and

19–20). King Saul was duly anointed. Thereafter, the unfaithfulness of Israel in demanding a king is largely forgotten, and the king became known as 'the Lord's anointed', although Jehovah was recognized as ultimately 'King of Zion' (e.g., Is. 33: 22; 41: 21; Jer. 8: 19 and Zech. 3: 15). This abiding sense of the kingship of God gave God's people a clear understanding of what true kingship involved and of how far short the majority of the kings of Israel and Judah fell of this ideal. King David's rule was the nearest approximation to it, yet even he was a poor representative of the perfect rule of heaven. It is not surprising therefore that, illumined by the Spirit of God, the psalmists and prophets looked forward to the day when God would again establish His own kingdom on earth, which would be 'Davidic', not only by reason of the king's ancestry, but also because it would perfectly exemplify the characteristics so imperfectly foreshadowed by David.

Four characteristics of this coming Kingdom stand out clearly. First, it would be just. Even David had sinned, and that grievously (2 Sam. 11–12), but the Messiah would have righteousness as 'the girdle of his loins' (Is. 11: 1–5) and would 'execute judgment and justice in the land' (Jer. 23: 5–6). Secondly, the Messiah's reign would usher in peace. David had 'waged great wars', and his son Solomon's very name was to typify the contrasting peace of his reign, 'for he shall be a man of peace' (1 Chron. 22: 6–10). So, during the Messiah's reign, 'Israel shall dwell safely' (Jer. 23: 1–6; Ezek. 34: 23–31). The third characteristic would be stability. David's throne was to be established for ever by 'an everlasting covenant' (2 Sam. 7: 10–16; Is. 55: 3). Fourthly, the Messianic Kingdom would be universal. David's kingdom had stretched 'from Dan to Beersheba'

(2 Sam. 3: 10), but ultimately God's promise to Abraham (Gen. 12: 3) would be fulfilled, that in his seed 'all the families of the earth' would be blessed. So, the coming Kingdom would extend not only to all ages but over all peoples. 'His dominion shall be from sea to sea, and from the river to the ends of the earth' (Zech. 9: 10).

These four characteristics of the future, ideal Kingdom are combined in Isaiah 9: 6–7. The kingdom of the boy to be born, as he sat 'on the throne of David', would be upheld 'with justice and righteousness'. His government would increase (i.e., spread). So would peace, and of both there would be no end. Indeed one may even discover these qualities in His splendid fourfold name, 'Wonderful Counsellor' (i.e., just ruler), 'Mighty God' (enjoying a universal dominion), 'Everlasting Father' and 'Prince of Peace'.

Such, in briefest outline, was the Old Testament expectation. In reference to it, Jesus said: 'the time has been fulfilled and the Kingdom of God has drawn near' (Mk. 1: 15). In comparing the fulfilment with the expectation, two special questions need to be answered, the first regarding the character of the Kingdom, and the second regarding its coming. Does the Kingdom of God as Jesus announced it exhibit the characteristics so clearly foretold? And when did it or will it come?

THE CHARACTER OF THE KINGDOM

There can be no doubt that Jesus was recognized by His contemporaries as at least a pretender to the Messianic throne. But the character of His Kingdom was widely different from that commonly envisaged. Its blessings were to be spiritual rather than material, and its glory was only to be revealed through suffering. It was this last point which the disciples were slow to understand and reluctant to believe, although it was foretold in the Scriptures, as Jesus repeatedly said. The servant of the Lord would suffer and bear His people's sins (Is. 52: 13–53). The shepherd would be smitten (Zech. 13: 7), and the house of Israel would look on Him whom they had pierced (12: 10). The Anointed One would be cut off (Dan. 9: 26). So Jesus kept referring to the Scriptures. 'The Son of man goes as it is written of Him' (Mk. 14: 21). 'Thus it is written, that the Christ should suffer and on the third day rise from the dead' (Lk. 24: 46). Once the disciples, through Simon Peter their spokesman, had confessed their faith in Him as the Messiah (Mk. 8: 27–30), Jesus began at once to teach them that 'the Son of man must suffer many things' (8: 31). Peter would not hear of it, but the Saviour rebuked him (8: 32–3) and kept teaching the same truth. The Son of man had come 'not to be ministered unto but to minister, and to give His life a ransom for many' (10: 32–45). The Good Shepherd would give His life, and that voluntarily, for His sheep (Jn. 10: 11, 18).

His mysterious action with bread and wine in the upper room dramatized His own statement that it was through His sacrificial death on the cross that forgiveness of sins was available and the New Covenant established (Mt. 26: 26–9). His Messiahship was thus revealed in fact and character to the disciples, but it was concealed from the people, lest they should accept the fact and misunderstand the character. The signs of the Kingdom were not to be blazoned abroad. The teaching of the Kingdom was private. This is the famous 'Messianic secret'. 'To you (that is, My disciples) it has been given to know the mysteries of the Kingdom, but to the rest in parables' (Mt. 13: 11). Only when the secret was out was the Kingdom's character made as plain as could be by a public fulfilment of Zechariah's prophecy (Zech. 9: 9; Mk. 11: 9–10; Jn. 12: 12–16) as He rode into the capital not on a prancing war charger as a military conqueror, but on a docile donkey as the the Prince of Peace.

The Kingdom of God in the teaching of Jesus is a spiritual conquest of men and women. It also has material benefits, since the King's subjects are the Father's children, and His sovereignty and paternity alike guarantee freedom from anxiety over food and clothing and the necessities of life. The heathen nations go in search of these things (Lk. 12: 30), but God's children possess them already, for they have entered His Kingdom (Mt. 6: 25–33; Lk. 12: 22–34). The Heavenly Father, for the final coming of whose Kingdom we pray, can be trusted to supply our daily bread (Mt. 6: 9–11; Lk. 11: 2–3). Nevertheless the Kingdom is not 'from this world' (Jn. 18: 36). 'The phrase', writes William Temple in his *Readings in St. John*, 'represents both origin and character due to origin.'[1] Its sphere is indeed this world, but its origin is divine and its character is the spread of the truth by which men are set free (Jn. 18: 37; 8: 32, 36). It is not imperialistic. It has no territorial rights or ambitions. Otherwise, the King's henchmen would fight. It works like leaven, conquering not by force from without but by grace from within (Mt. 13: 33). It is, to use T. W. Manson's forceful words, 'something through and through spiritual'. 'It is a personal relation between God and the individual human being.'[2]

The story of the rich young ruler illustrates clearly

---

[1] *Readings in St. John*, by W. Temple, p. 353 (Macmillan, 1945.)
[2] *The Teaching of Jesus*, by T. W. Manson, p. 132. (Cambridge University Press, 1935.)
B

the spiritual nature of the Kingdom of God. He came asking how he might inherit eternal life (Mk. 10: 17). Jesus answered his question and then spoke about the difficulty of entering the Kingdom of God (10: 23–5), while the disciples finally enquired: 'Are there few that be saved?' (10: 26). From this and similar evidence throughout the gospel narratives it is difficult to resist the conclusion that to have eternal life, to be saved and to be a citizen of the Kingdom of God are one and the same thing. So, too, the compilers of our Book of Common Prayer understood the matter, for in the Baptism Service they state that Christ's promise signified in that sacrament is 'to receive him, to release him of his sins, to sanctify him with the Holy Ghost, to give him the Kingdom of heaven, and everlasting life' (The Ministration of Public Baptism to Infants).

Such in general terms is the character of the Messianic Kingdom as announced by Jesus Christ. It is necessary now to consider how far the four recurrent characteristics observed in Old Testament prophecy have been fulfilled. They all undoubtedly find their place in our Lord's description of the Kingdom, but, as we should expect, the fulfilment is richer than the expectation and transcends the thought-forms of all the Old Testament anticipation. There is in fact in each characteristic a significant alteration of emphasis.

Righteousness is an obvious mark of the Kingdom in the New Testament as in the Old, but whereas in the Old Testament it is the King's righteous rule which is described, in the New Testament it is the righteousness of the King's subjects which receives the emphasis. Moral repentance is the first condition of entry into the Kingdom (Mk. 1: 15), involving not just the profession of the lips but the obedience of the life (Mt. 7: 21 *et seqq.*).

The righteousness of members of the Kingdom must exceed that of the Scribes and Pharisees, and the measure of their obedience to the new law will be the measure of their greatness in the new Kingdom (Mt. 5: 17–20). Righteousness is not, however, always an altogether 'moral' concept in the gospels. It also suggests that 'legal' acceptance which the apostle Paul was later to expound. It is to be 'sought', and that with 'hunger and thirst' (Mt. 5: 6; 6: 33) as a gift of God's grace rather than as an achievement of man's effort. That is why the publican went down to his house 'pronounced righteous' rather than the self-righteous Pharisee (Lk. 18: 14).

Peace is a second clear characteristic of the Kingdom, as Jesus described it. The word was frequently on His lips. But again there is a difference. The material symbolism of the Old Testament expectation is fulfilled in a moral quality. It takes two forms, corresponding to the two aspects of the prophetic anticipation. Firstly, anticipated freedom from the fear of war is realized through carefree trust in the Heavenly Father. 'Take no anxious thought!' The Father-King feeds the ravens, clothes the lilies, protects the sparrows, and counts your hairs. Let faith banish fear (Mt. 6: 25–34; Lk. 12: 22–31). Secondly, the prediction of peaceful civil relationships finds its fulfilment in the harmony of the Christian brotherhood. The sons of the Kingdom are not to judge one another, but to love one another and to forgive one another (Mt. 18: 15–35, where 'brother' occurs three times).

It is interesting to note that these two primary marks of the Kingdom are both mentioned in the Beatitudes, where blessedness is promised both to those who hunger and thirst after righteousness and to the peacemakers (Mt. 5: 6, 9; cf. Rom. 14: 17). 'Righteousness and peace have kissed each other' (Ps. 85:10).

The third expected characteristic of the Kingdom was stability. So it is stated before our Lord's birth that He will 'reign over the house of Jacob for ever' (Lk. 1: 33). The significant difference in emphasis, however, lies in the process of the Kingdom's coming. The Old Testament seers, with that foreshortening of vision which is a characteristic of predictive prophesy, announced the sudden establishment of a stable and everlasting Kingdom. Jesus, however, as will be shown later, proclaimed a Kingdom which comes in lowliness, grows in extent across the years and will only be consummated at the end of the ages.

Universality is the fourth anticipated mark of the Messianic Kingdom, and this is clearly fulfilled in the teaching of Jesus. The change of emphasis concerns the place occupied respectively by the Jews and the Gentiles. In the Old Testament prediction, the Messianic Kingdom is, of course, to be supremely the restored Kingdom of Israel–Judah, in which the Gentiles will be granted a place. But according to the New Testament fulfilment many of the chosen race will be excluded from the Kingdom, whose doors will be thrown open not to the proud religious leaders but to the despised outcasts, not to the privileged, unbelieving Jews, but to the unprivileged, believing Gentiles. 'I tell you, many will come from east and west and sit at table with Abraham, Isaac and Jacob in the Kingdom of Heaven, while the sons of the Kingdom (that is, the Jews) will be thrown into the outer darkness' (Mt. 8: 11–12; Lk. 13: 28–30). The mustard seed will grow into a large shrub, big enough for birds to rest in its shade (Mk. 4: 32) and nest in its branches (Mt. 13: 32; Lk. 13: 19). The yeast will leaven the whole dough, even if the three measures of meal do not typify (as some ancient commentators suggested) Shem, Ham and Japheth, the three sons of Noah! Thus the risen Lord declared that all authority was His on earth as in heaven, and that therefore His Church was to go and make disciples of all nations and be His witnesses unto the uttermost parts of the earth (Mt. 28: 18–19; Acts 1: 8). It is this last characteristic of the Kingdom which enthralled the mind of Luke, the doctor evangelist, as we shall see in the next chapter.

THE COMING OF THE KINGDOM

If this is the character of the Messianic Kingdom, clearly portrayed in the expectation but enriched in the fulfilment, when did the Kingdom come? The question has been the subject of much debate. Some scholars have maintained that the Kingdom came once and for all with Jesus, and that the 'last things' had arrived. This is the school of so-called 'realized eschatology'. Others have declared that the teaching of Jesus was entirely futuristic and belonged exclusively to the next age. The controversy has been unnecessarily complicated by a tendency to forget that in the New Testament as a whole the conception of the Kingdom is not a static one. There was no one moment in the triumphant progress of our saving Lord from His cradle in Bethlehem to His final glory at the Father's right hand, at which it may be said 'the Kingdom came or will come then.' The Kingdom was coming all the time. It is still growing. Its progress is twofold, first as God gives it, and second as man receives it.

THE DIVINE UNFOLDING

There is a sense in which the Kingdom never began, since it has a direct historical continuity with the old

Kingdom. There is another sense in which the Bethlehem manger was the King's first throne, resplendent with the glory of His incarnation. But in the mind of Jesus and the evangelists the Kingdom began to come at the Baptism. It was the Messiah's anointing. The voice from heaven employed words from the Messianic psalm (2: 7): 'Thou art my beloved Son.' So Jesus could immediately say 'the time has been fulfilled; the Kingdom of God has drawn near.' Probably He did not say 'the Kingdom of God has arrived', because it still needed to be accepted by men. So He added: 'Repent and believe in the good news' (Mk. 1: 15). That the Kingdom had really in one sense 'come', however, is clear from the fact that He implied the possibility of entering it then and there. The Scribes and Pharisees were blocking the road into the Kingdom (Mt. 23:13), but the crowds were 'taking it by force' (Mt. 11: 12). Further and stronger evidence for the Kingdom's presence, to which Jesus Himself pointed, is to be found in His mighty works of healing. They were the signs of the Kingdom. The Kingdom of Satan was retreating before the advancing Kingdom of the Messiah, for 'if it is by the finger of God that I cast out demons, then the Kingdom of God has come upon you' (Mt. 12: 22–30; Lk. 11: 14–23). Jesus finally disposed of any doubt as to the present aspect of the Kingdom when, in answer to the Pharisee's enquiring 'when the Kingdom of God was coming', He replied: 'the Kingdom of God comes not by calculation . . . the Kingdom of God is among you.' That is, the final coming of the Kingdom would not be dated by careful calculation. Meanwhile, the present coming has taken place and escaped their notice! It is not localized at all. Men cannot say: 'Lo, here! lo, there!' for it was already in their very midst (Lk. 17: 20–1).

The second manifestation of the Kingdom was the Transfiguration. When Peter, having confessed his faith in Jesus as Messiah, went on to object that He must not be allowed to suffer, Jesus declared that the Son of man who should suffer on the cross (Mk. 8: 31) was the Son of man who should come with the clouds (8: 38). Meanwhile, some of them would be granted a glimpse before death of the glory of His Kingdom (9: 1). This 'exceptional privilege of some as distinct from the common experience of all'[1] was granted to Peter, James and John on the holy mount, when they saw Jesus transfigured with glory. The evangelists, by telling the story of the Transfiguration immediately, show plainly that they understood Jesus' words to refer to this event. This is the common patristic interpretation of a difficult verse. The Transfiguration was a striking manifestation of the Son of man in His Kingdom, and again the voice of acclamation was heard from heaven.

The third stage in the establishment of the Kingdom took place on the cross. Golgotha's tree was as much a throne as Bethlehem's manger. In the temptation following His baptism He had committed Himself to the conquest of the kingdoms of the world by the way of the Cross (Mt. 4: 8; Lk. 4: 5). When the sons of Zebedee asked for the chief seats in the Kingdom He immediately spoke of the bitter cup and baptism by which the Kingdom would be attained (Mt. 10: 35–45). The temple of His physical body had to be destroyed before the temple of His spiritual body could be raised and the Temple of His mystical Body, the Church, be built (Jn. 2: 19–22). During the last supper He spoke of His Kingdom in which the Messianic banquet would be enjoyed, but said He would not take part in it until His death had

[1] *St. Luke*, by A. Plummer. (T. & T. Clark, 1896.)

fulfilled the symbolism of both the Passover and the cup (Mk. 4: 25; Mt. 26: 29; Lk. 22: 16, 18). The Covenant-Kingdom with its offer of forgiveness, could only be ratified by His blood (Mt. 26: 28; Lk. 22: 29). Indeed, according to St. John, Jesus described His death as His glorification and His 'lifting up'. When the Greeks asked to see Him, He said: 'The hour has come for the Son of man to be glorified' and went on immediately to speak of His death (Jn. 12: 20–32), concluding (12: 32) 'I, if I be lifted up from the earth, will draw all men unto Me.' To see Him crucified would be to see Him glorified. Only when the King was enthroned on His cross would all men flock into His Kingdom. It was the seed that died which multiplied (12: 24).

The Kingdom came at the Baptism, at the Transfiguration, at the cross. The Kingdom also came at the Resurrection and Exaltation. Jesus never predicted His passion without adding that He would rise (Mk. 8: 31; 9: 31; 10: 34). During the forty days which elapsed between His resurrection and His ascension, He spoke 'concerning the Kingdom of God' (Acts 1: 3), which suggests that by His death and resurrection the Kingdom had entered on a new phase. The apostles were quite clear about this. 'God has made Him both Lord and Christ, this Jesus whom you crucified', cried Peter on the day of Pentecost (Acts 2: 24–36). This, too, is a theme of the Pauline epistles (cf. Phil. 2: 7–11) and of the Epistle to the Hebrews where the ascended Christ is the priest-king (8: 1).

Pentecost was a further manifestation of the Kingdom's coming. The Holy Spirit was the 'great gift of our ascended King'. Our Lord's sequence of thought in Acts 1: 3–8 is very enlightening. He spoke to them during the forty days about the Kingdom of God. On the Mount of Olives the disciples asked Him, 'wilt Thou at this time restore the Kingdom to Israel?' (1: 6). As Calvin wrote, there are almost as many errors as words in their question! They revealed a threefold misunderstanding about the Kingdom. First, they were mistaken about the *time* of its manifestation. They were not to know. The Father had fixed the times and the seasons by His own authority (1: 7). Secondly, they were mistaken about its *sphere*. They asked if He would restore the Kingdom to Israel. He replied that they would be witnesses unto the uttermost parts of the earth (1: 8). Thirdly, they were mistaken about its *character*. They appear still to have been thinking in terms of a material domain. He told them of a spiritual dominion. The Kingdom would spread as the Spirit gave them power for witness to Christ (1: 8). The same Spirit who cast out demons in the ministry of Jesus (Mt. 12: 28) would cause the Kingdom to spread as He bore witness through the apostles to the unbelieving world (Jn. 15: 25–6).

Another undoubted manifestation of the Kingdom's coming was the destruction of Jerusalem by the Roman legions under the command of the Emperor Titus in A.D. 70. Jesus clearly foretold this event in His great apocalyptic discourse recorded in Mark 13, Matthew 24 and Luke 21 (especially vv. 20–4, 31), although the passage is confusing because references to this event and to His final coming in judgment are interwoven. The destruction of Jerusalem was a coming of the Kingdom partly because in it the King rose up in judgment upon His miscreant citizens (Mt. 21: 40–3; 22: 5–7) and partly because He thereby confirmed finally His giving of the Kingdom to the Gentiles (Mt. 21: 43). By it the Church was delivered from a lingering Judaism and set free on its great missionary advance into the Gentile world. The destruction of Jerusalem was a miniature of the King's final coming in judgment (Mk. 13: 1–4), just as the Transfiguration was a miniature of His final coming in glory.

We have now distinguished four principal phases in the manifestation of the Kingdom, namely, at the beginning, in the middle, at the end and after the end of the ministry of Jesus. At the Baptism and Temptation the Kingdom of God is declared and tested. At Peter's confession, the first Passion-prediction and the Transfiguration it is recognized by man, defined by Jesus and confirmed by God. At the cross the character of the Kingdom is finally demonstrated, and by the Resurrection and Ascension it is vindicated. The cross fulfils the foreshadowings of the Temptation and Passion-prediction, as the Resurrection and Exaltation fulfil the Baptism and Transfiguration voices. Now established, the Kingdom's two aspects of grace and wrath are revealed at Pentecost and the Destruction of Jerusalem, both of which are to be consummated at the end of the age. The final coming of Christ or 'parousia', will fulfil all these foreshadowings and complete all these partial comings.

So the disciples are still to pray: 'Thy Kingdom come' (Mt. 6: 10; Lk. 11: 2). The present sowing and growth await the final harvest. The householder and doorkeeper and virgins must wait and watch. The day will be heralded by signs, but its appearing will eventually be sudden and unexpected. He will become simultaneously manifest to the whole world, as the lightning flashes across the sky (Mt. 24: 27; Lk. 17: 24). It will be a day of separation. 'One will be taken and the other left' (Mt. 24: 40–1; Lk. 17: 31–5). The King will sit on the throne of His glory and separate the nations, as a shepherd separates the sheep from the goats (Mt. 25: 31–46). Then will come the final *dénouement*, and the Kingdom will be inherited by those for whom it has been prepared from the foundation of the world (v. 34). The Kingdom will have been consummated.

These are the successive stages by which the Kingdom may be said to have 'come'. What, however, it has been necessary to distinguish linguistically and historically, it is not necessary to distinguish theologically. God established His Kingdom through the first advent of His Christ. The Baptism, Transfiguration, Crucifixion, Resurrection, Exaltation, and Gift of the Spirit were all aspects of the one deed of redemption and the one establishment of the Kingdom. Now the Kingdom spreads, not only as God gives it but as man receives it.

THE HUMAN DEVELOPMENT

Jesus clearly taught that the extension of the Kingdom was dependent on the response which men and women make to its moral demands. The parables collected together in the thirteenth chapter of Matthew's gospel illustrate this growth from different aspects. 'If the mustard seed declares the extensive, the leaven declares the intensive, development of the gospel.'[1] But in the Parable of the Sower, the yield of the crops depends on the condition of the soil. The birds, the sun and the thorns can prevent the seed from bearing fruit. If the Parable of the Sower portrays some in whose lives the Kingdom is never properly received, the Parables of the Treasure and the Pearl describe those who count everything else loss in comparison with the great gain of obtaining the Kingdom.

What, then, are the conditions of entry into the

[1] *Notes on the Parables of Our Lord*, by R. C. Trench. (Routledge, 1902.)

Kingdom? The Kingdom is 'given' (Lk. 12: 32, cf. Mt. 21: 43)—in order to be received or rejected (Mk. 10: 15). How can it be entered? The Lord's statement to Nico-demus was clear: 'Unless a man be born from above he cannot see the Kingdom of God' (Jn. 3: 3). The new birth is not identical with baptism, although baptism is its sign and seal. It is a deep, inward, revolutionary change of heart effected by the Holy Spirit. Without it a man cannot even 'see' the Kingdom, let alone 'enter' it (3: 3, 5). But how can this change come about? On what human conditions will the Holy Spirit effect it? <u>The first is implied in the context. It is repentance.</u> 'Except a man be born of water and of the Spirit, he cannot enter the Kingdom of heaven' (3: 5). Birth of water can only have meant one thing to Nicodemus. 'The words have a distinct historical meaning.'[1] They must refer to John's baptism, for John was himself dis-tinguishing between his own water-baptism and the coming Messiah's 'Spirit-baptism' (Jn. 1: 31–3). Now, John's baptism was a baptism of repentance (Mk. 1: 4–5). Jesus' first word of command, after the announcement of the Kingdom's approach, was 'Repent!' (1: 15). He had come 'to call sinners to repentance' (Mk. 2: 17; Lk. 5: 32). This was the first condition of entry into the Kingdom. One particular sin to be renounced was the unforgiving spirit (Mt. 6: 14–15; 18: 15–35; Mk. 11: 25). Further it is in this connexion that His teaching about 'offences' should be mentioned. The offending hand, foot or eye, which are to be cut off and plucked out if they hinder entry into the Kingdom, are probably off-ending practices which cannot be retained if Kingdom-membership is desired (Mk. 9: 42–8).

[1] *The Gospel According to St. John,* ad loc. by B. F. Westcott. (Murray, 1919).

Faith is the second condition of entry into the Kingdom. If Jesus' first word was 'Repent', His second was 'Believe in the good news'. It was not just the fact of the good news which He made the object of man's faith, but His own person. Men were to believe in Him. Unbelief hindered Him from performing the signs of the Kingdom (Mk. 6: 5–6). He required faith in those who sought His healing (e.g., Mk. 9: 14–29). It was not only for the healing of the body, however, that faith was necessary. St. John records more particularly the necessity of believing 'into' or 'onto' Christ with personal trust and self-committal if eternal life is to be received (e.g., 6: 47). Once in the synoptic gospels is a disciple described as 'he that believeth in Me' (Mt. 18: 6), but the phrase is common in the fourth gospel.

The third condition of entry into the Kingdom is self-surrender. 'If any man will come after Me, let him deny himself and take up his cross and follow Me' (Mk. 8: 34). There must be a willingness to 'lose oneself', to 'die', to follow Jesus to crucifixion, to abdicate the throne of one's life. It may mean the renunciation of possessions (Mt. 19: 23–6; Mk. 10: 23–7; Lk. 18: 24–7). It may mean the renunciation of family (Mt. 10: 37). It always means the renunciation of self. No wonder He urged would-be followers to count the cost (Lk. 14: 25–33) and warned them that the gate was narrow (Mt. 7: 14; Lk. 13: 24). The pearl merchant, like the discoverer of the treasure, had to sell 'all that he had' (the phrase is repeated in both parables) in order to secure the prize (Mt. 13: 44–5). 'So likewise, whosoever he be of you that forsaketh not lla that he hath, he cannot be My disciple' (Lk. 14: 33).

This claim on our total allegiance is one which we all need to face squarely to-day. Jesus never encouraged half-hearted discipleship. He asked for all or nothing.

And in asking for all, He did not ask more than He was prepared to give Himself. He asked a cross for a cross, and a life for a life.

In all these conditions, the little child supplied Him with the best illustration. The child is humble enough to trust and obey, to receive gifts and to submit to authority. 'Verily I say unto you, unless you turn and become like children, you will never enter the Kingdom of heaven. Whosoever humbles himself like this child, he is the greatest in the Kingdom of heaven' (Mt. 18: 3–4). The Kingdom belongs to the childlike (Mk. 10: 13–15).

Such self-denial is true self-discovery. 'Whosoever will save his life shall lose it, but whosoever shall lose his life for My sake and the gospel's, the same shall save it' (Mk. 8: 35). 'The disciple is not above his Lord', and the greatest privilege of the citizen of the Kingdom is to follow in the footsteps of the lowly King who girded Himself with a towel, washed His disciples' feet (Jn. 13: 1–17), moved among men 'as he that serveth' (Lk. 22: 27), and finally gave 'His life a ransom for many' (Mk. 10: 45).

Chapter II

THE MESSAGE OF LUKE

All flesh shall see the salvation of God.—Luke 2: 6

HAVING considered the principal themes of the teaching of Jesus (as set forth mostly in St. Mark's Gospel and in the material common to Matthew and Luke), it is natural to turn to St. Luke. His is in many ways the most distinctive of the three synoptic gospels, and, since he is the author of the Acts of the Apostles as well, his literary contribution to the New Testament is greater than that of any other writer (more than a quarter of the whole). It is clearly the fourth characteristic of the Kingdom of God which dominated his outlook, namely, its universality, and for the elaboration of this theme he was particularly fitted.

(1) *Luke was a Gentile.* Indeed, he was the only Gentile among the writers of the New Testament. This is now generally accepted. Thus, when Paul sends greetings to the Colossian Christians he mentions three of his companions by name as 'the only men of the circumcision among my fellow workers for the Kingdom of God'. He goes on to send greetings from three others, who are presumably not Jewish. Among them is 'Luke the beloved physician' (Col. 4: 10–14). If one tradition is to be trusted, he was 'an Antiochian of Syria', and if the Bezan text of Acts 11: 28 is correct, using the first person plural ('when we assembled together'), Luke was in Antioch at that time. Certainly he displays in

23

Acts a considerable knowledge of the inner life of the
Antiochene Church (11: 19–27; 13: 1; 14: 19–26; 15:
22–5; 18: 22). Now Antioch was the capital of Syria,
'the Queen of the East', 'the third metropolis of the
Roman Empire'. That Luke was a Greek-speaking
Gentile is further suggested by the fact that whenever
he quotes from the Old Testament he uses the Greek
version and does not translate direct from the Hebrew.
Hebrew is in fact 'their language' (Acts 1: 19) not 'ours'.
Further corroboration of his Greek background is
supplied by his portraiture of Jesus as the ideal man.
'The most fervent passion of the best Greek idealism
and philosophy was for the perfecting of human personality.'[1] It is suggested that Luke found this ideal in Jesus,
and so laid more emphasis than the other evangelists on
His life of service to man and of prayer to God.

(2) *Luke was a doctor.* He is so called by St. Paul in
the passage already quoted and Paul adds the epithet
'beloved' no doubt because Luke had tended him when
he was suffering from the malady to which he refers in
Galatians 4: 12–15 and which was probably the 'thorn
in the flesh' of 2 Corinthians 12: 7. In 1882 a book was
written by W. K. Hobart entitled *The Medical Language
of St. Luke*.[2] In his introduction he explains that the
purpose of his book was to show that both the gospel
and the Acts 'are the works of a person well acquainted
with the language of the Greek medical schools'. He
proceeds, very laboriously and somewhat uncritically, to
catalogue over four hundred special Lucan words which
are also used by the Greek medical writers Hippocrates,
Aretæus, Galen, and Dioscorides. Later scholars have

[1] *Commentary on the Gospel of Luke*, by Norval Geldenhuys, p. 45
(Marshall, Morgan & Scott, 1950.)
[2] Dublin University Press.

shown his case to be very much weaker than he supposed, but there is still enough evidence to prove Luke's medical interests. Some incidents reported by all three synoptists are given a specially medical flavour by Luke. Thus, Peter's mother-in-law was not just 'sick of a fever' (as Matthew and Mark say), but 'holden with a great fever' (4: 38). The one who came seeking cleansing was not just 'a leper' (as Matthew and Mark are content to describe him) but 'a man full of leprosy' (5: 12). Again, in relating the story of the woman with an issue of blood, Luke, no doubt from motives of professional jealousy, declines to say with Mark that she 'had suffered many things of many physicians and had spent all that she had, and was nothing bettered, but rather grew worse' (Mk. 5: 26; Lk. 8: 43). It is also only he who records the fact that Jesus in the Nazareth synagogue quoted the proverb: 'Physician, heal thyself' (4: 23).

(3) *Luke was an educated man*. He would need to be as a physician. Plummer even writes[1] in connexion with Luke's knowledge of Paul, 'It is not improbable that it was at Tarsus, where there was a school of philosophy and literature rivalling those of Alexandria and Athens that they first met. Luke may have studied medicine at Tarsus. Nowhere else in Asia Minor could he obtain so good an education.' His culture is clearly seen in his books. He has a very rich vocabulary, with about eight hundred words in Luke and the Acts which do not occur elsewhere in the New Testament. Renan calls his Gospel '*le plus beau livre qu'il y ait*', and J. M. Creed, one of the most recent commentators on the Gospel (1930), speaks of the 'irreproachable literary Greek' of his preface, and the conscious artistry which enables him to change to the more Hebraic Greek of the infancy narratives. 'The

[1] *St. Luke*, by A. Plummer, pp. xx–xxi. (T. & T. Clark, 1896.)
C

author of the third gospel and of the Acts is the most versatile of all the New Testament writers.'[1] A tradition which cannot be traced beyond the sixth or eighth century A.D. affirms that Luke was an artist and had painted the portrait of the Virgin Mary. The evidence is highly doubtful, but that he is an artist in words none will dispute.

(4) *Luke was a historian.* He is not content to describe the ministry of John or of Jesus in the setting of Palestine alone. He sees it in the wider context of the Roman Empire. 'One of the most impressive features of the early chapters of the gospel is the elaborate synchronism with which Luke marks the beginning of the ministry of John (3: 1-2). This synchronism, together with a number of somewhat less elaborate historical and chronological data in Luke, have strongly contributed to the judgment that Luke is the historian among the evangelists. He reflects indeed the consciousness that the events he narrates concern a movement which found expression, not in some remote corner of the world, but in the midst of the Roman Empire in the full light of day—within the framework of world history.'[2] Luke has been vindicated in recent years as an accurate and painstaking historian, and he includes in his two volumes many references to Roman provincial administration and to the secular and political affairs of his day. 'Luke's history is unsurpassed in respect of its trustworthiness.'[3] Certainly he claims, in his preface to the gospel (1: 1-4), that he had carefully investigated his sources, both written and oral, before venturing to compile his own ordered gospel narrative.

[1] Plummer, op. cit., p. xlix.
[2] *The Witness of Luke to Christ*, by N. B. Stonehouse, pp. 58-9. (Tyndale Press, 1951.)
[3] *The Bearing of Recent Discovery on the Trustworthiness of the New Testament*, by Sir W. M. Ramsay, p. 80. (Hodder & Stoughton, 1915.)

(5) *Luke was a traveller*. It is known that he travelled with the apostle Paul on at least three occasions. Besides this, he must have travelled on his own account. He betrays an intimate knowledge of local affairs, Roman, Greek, Jewish, and Christian, which suggests the familiarity of a much-travelled man. He had sailed on the Mediterranean and Ægean seas, so that to him the sea of Galilee was only a 'lake', and his use of nautical terms in describing the shipwreck (Acts 27) led Farrar[1] to suggest that he had been a ship's doctor!

(6) *Luke was Paul's companion*. All students of the Acts will know that three times in his narrative Luke, the author, changes from the third personal plural 'they' to the first person plural 'we', to signify thus modestly that he was himself present. On the first occasion he accompanies Paul on the epoch-making voyage into Europe, setting sail with him and Silas and Timothy from Troas, and journeying to Philippi (16: 10–18). There he is evidently left behind, when the others move on, as the first 'we' section ends. The second does not begin until 20: 5. The scene is again Philippi. Paul is now homeward bound on his third missionary journey. He picks up Luke, and they travel together to Jerusalem. The second 'we' section ends with 21: 18, on their arrival. Paul is arrested and later transferred to Caesarea. Here Luke rejoins him and finally accompanies him on the long and eventful voyage to Rome (27: 1–28: 16). Tertullian speaks of him as being 'inseparable from Paul', and he may very well have remained loyally at the great Apostle's side until the end. Certainly, Paul's three references to Luke in his epistles show that he was with him in Rome, Colossians 4: 10–14 and Philemon

[1] *St. Luke*, by F. W. Farrar, p. 21. (Cambridge Bible for Schools and Colleges, 1885.)

24 written during the first imprisonment, and 2 Timothy
4: 11 ('only Luke is with me') during the second. This
close association of Luke with Paul cannot have failed
to influence the evangelist's outlook. His Gospel may
be expected to reflect the teaching of Paul, as Mark's
does that of Peter.

Such is the man whom the Holy Spirit was preparing
to contribute more than a quarter of the whole New
Testament. He was a man of the world—of the large
Graeco-Roman world of his day. For what did his
Gentile background, his professional experience, his
literary and historical gifts, his travels and his association with Paul equip him? There can be no doubt as to
the answer to this question. Luke was a man of wide
views and broad sympathies. His natural love for the
afflicted had led him into medicine. His Gentile origin,
his experiences in travel and his historical sense
enabled him to see the gospel in its world setting.
Paul's influence must have filled his mind with the
message of free salvation offered to all irrespective
of privilege. Luke was the man chosen and fitted by
the Holy Spirit to lay emphasis on the universality of
the Gospel.

He wrote a two-volume work on the origins of
Christianity. It describes the work of Jesus in the world,
now incarnate (in the Gospel), now risen but working
still through His Spirit (in the Acts). 'In the Gospel we
see the Christ winning salvation for the whole world;
in the Acts we see His apostles carrying the good tidings
of this salvation to the whole world.'[1] It is a single work,
the preface to the Gospel covering both sections,[2] and

[1] Plummer, op. cit., p. xxxvi.
[2] Stonehouse, op. cit., pp. 11–13.

it is a book by a Gentile for Gentiles. He shows quite clearly that Christianity is rooted in the Old Testament, but whereas Matthew goes out of his way to show how minutely the saving career of Jesus fulfilled Scripture, Luke omits nearly all quotations except such as came from the lips of the Lord Himself. He either leaves out Aramaic words employed by Matthew and Mark, or else replaces them by their Greek equivalent. Thus 'Simon the Canaanæan' becomes 'Simon the Zealot', 'Abba Father' becomes just 'Father', 'the place Golgotha which is being interpreted A skull' becomes 'the place which is called The Skull'. He also reduces the thirty occurrences in Matthew of 'Amen I say unto you' to only seven, and explains some Jewish customs, e.g., 'The feast of unleavened bread—which is called the Passover' (22: 1).

Both volumes are addressed to one 'Theophilus' (Lk. 1: 3; Acts 1: 1). The Greek word means 'loved by God' or 'dear to God', and from earliest days commentators have suggested that it might symbolize every earnest Christian reader. The addition of the epithet 'most excellent' (Lk. 1: 3), however, suggests that a definite person was in mind, a Gentile of some rank (cf. the use of the term in Acts 23: 26; 24: 3; 26: 25). B. H. Streeter[1] says that 'the name Theophilus in the Lucan prefaces looks like a prudential pseudonym for some Roman of position', and goes on to make the fascinating suggestion that none other than T. Flavius Clemens was intended. He was the Emperor Domitian's cousin by marriage, and was heir apparent. His wife Domitilla is known to have been a Christian, and there is evidence to suggest that Clemens was too. 'Indeed, it is not impossible that Theophilus was the secret name by which Flavius

[1] *The Four Gospels*, by B. H. Streeter, p. 534. (Macmillan, 1924.)

Clemens was known in the Roman Church.'[1] This is a very ingenious conjecture, but lacks solid proof. Whoever Theophilus was, he stands as 'a representative Gentile convert'.[2]

The great theme therefore of both Gospel and Acts, of which nearly every discourse and incident is a variation, is that the good news of Jesus Christ is universal in its application. It includes all sorts and conditions of men in its wide embrace. Close to the opening of the Gospel comes the quotation from Isaiah 40: 3–5, illustrating the ministry of John the Baptist. All four evangelists include it, but only Luke continues the quotation to include the significant phrase 'and all flesh shall see the salvation of God' (Lk. 3: 6). Close to the beginning of Acts, in the course of his sermon on the day of Pentecost, Peter quotes from Joel equally significant words: 'I will pour out My Spirit upon all flesh' (Acts 2: 17). These two references to the inclusion of 'all flesh' within the offer of salvation stand like signposts at the beginning of each volume to point the way. Similarly when giving the genealogy of Jesus, he traces His ancestry not only to Abraham, the father of the Jewish family (as Matthew does), but to Adam, the founder of the human race (Lk. 3: 38). Luke appears to go out of his way to demonstrate that the ministry of Jesus and His apostles was exercised to all in need, whatever their race or rank, for every mortal creature was the object of God's grace. It is striking to observe his particular interest in different classes of person, who might have been thought to have been excluded.

(1) *Children.* The exposure of children was a not uncommon practice in the Roman empire. It was the

[1] ibid., p. 539.
[2] Plummer, op. cit., p. xxxiii.

Christians who founded homes for orphans and waifs and strays. They did so because of the Lord's love for children, and this Luke clearly sees. The incomparable story of the annunciation to Elizabeth and Mary, and the visit of Mary to the Judean hills to see Elizabeth when both were pregnant is a story which belongs only to Luke. Only he goes on to describe the birth of Jesus in the Bethlehem stable, the angelic visitants to the neighbouring fields and the visit of the shepherds to greet the Holy Child. He then tells of the circumcision of Jesus and of His presentation in the Temple. He has preserved for us the only Gospel story of our Lord's boyhood, and casts the only light we are given on the silent years before this incident (2: 40) and after it (2: 52) by saying that He was growing in body, in wisdom and in spirit. The three synoptic evangelists tell us of His love for children during His ministry, but only Luke writes of the widow of Nain who lost her son (Lk. 7: 11–17) and that Jairus' daughter was an 'only' daughter (8: 42) and that the lunatic boy was an 'only' child (9: 38). Matthew and Mark tell how they brought 'little children' to Jesus that He should touch them, but it is Luke who describes them by the even tenderer name 'babies' (18: 15). Matthew and Mark both record that, in order to teach humility, Jesus took a little child and set him in the midst, but Luke alone adds the homely touch that He set him 'by His side' (9: 47).

(2) *Women*. Women were despised in the Roman Empire, and contemporary Jewish thought was equally contemptuous. One of the daily Rabbinic thanksgivings was: 'Blessed be Thou, O Lord God, who hast not made me a woman.' 'The Scribes and Pharisees gathered up their robes in the streets and synagogues lest they should touch a woman, and held it a crime to look on an un-

veiled woman in public.'[1] Very different was the
Christian attitude. It was already in his epistle to the
Galatians, probably his first epistle, that St. Paul had
made the tremendous statement 'there is neither male
nor female, for you are all one in Christ Jesus' (3: 28).
Luke may therefore have been influenced by Paul, but
his own views were doubtless formed from his knowledge of our Lord's attitude. St. Luke's Gospel is the
gospel of womanhood, and tells more than the others
the gracious, courteous attitude of Jesus towards women,
and the place He allowed them to occupy in His
ministry. It is he who tells, with such delicate reserve,
the story of the miraculous conception and birth of
Jesus. Mary, the mother of Jesus, and Elizabeth, the
mother of the Baptist, were kinswomen, and the story
must have been derived directly or indirectly from Mary
herself. The other evangelists tell the stories of the
woman with the issue of blood, Jairus' daughter, Peter's
sick mother-in-law, and the Bethany anointing, but only
Luke writes of the prophetess Anna (2: 36–8), of the
widow of Nain (7: 11–17), of the woman who was a
sinner (7: 36–50), of the ministering women (8: 2–3),
of Martha and Mary (10: 38–42), of the woman whom
Satan had bound for eighteen years (13: 10–17), and
of the daughters of Jerusalem who wept (23: 27–31).
Similarly, in the Acts he refers several times to the fact
that 'multitudes both of men and women' embraced the
gospel (5: 14; cf. 1: 14; 8: 3; 17: 4 and 12). He also tells
of Tabitha, whom Peter brought back to life in Joppa
(9: 36–43), and of Lydia and the slave girl, who were
converted during the mission in Philippi (16: 12–18
and 40).

(3) *The Sick*. The healing work of Jesus was such a

[1] Farrar, op. cit., p. 27.

prominant feature of His ministry that all the evangelists lay great emphasis on it, but Luke more than the
others. Some details reflecting his professional interest
as a doctor have already been mentioned, but there is
more evidence still to suggest that this tender-hearted
man felt the compassion of Jesus towards suffering
humanity. The parable of the Good Samaritan is recorded by Luke only (10: 25–37). Reference has already
been made to his account of the healing of the woman
who 'had a spirit of infirmity for eighteen years' and
'was bent over and could not fully straighten herself'
(13: 10–17). Only Luke records the Lord's cure of the
man with dropsy (14: 2), and only he mentions what
Plummer[1] called the 'surgical miracle' of the healing of
Malchus' ear (22: 50–1). He reveals a special sympathy
for lepers. Partly because of their loathsome symptoms
and the dangers of infection and partly because they
were popularly supposed to be under the divine curse,
the Pharisees used to throw stones at them to make them
keep their distance. The evangelists tell us, however,
that Jesus 'stretched forth His hand and touched' the
leper who came to Him. Luke adds that this man was
'full of leprosy' (5: 12), and is the only one to record
the healing of the ten lepers (17: 11–19). In the Acts,
the continuation of Jesus' healing ministry through the
hands of the apostles (5: 12; 14: 3) is described. Peter
and John heal the congenital cripple at the beautiful
gate of the Temple, 'in the name of Jesus Christ of
Nazareth' (3: 1–4: 22). Peter cures Æneas at Lydda,
who 'had been bedridden for eight years and was para-
lysed', addressing to him the confident words: 'Æneas,
Jesus Christ heals you; rise and make your bed' (9: 32–5).
Philip healed many sufferers in Samaria, bringing much

[1] Plummer, op. cit., p. lxv.

joy to the city (8: 4–8). So active was the Lord's healing grace that it is said to have operated even through Peter's shadow in Jerusalem (5: 15–16) and Paul's handkerchief in Ephesus (19: 11–12). Paul also healed a poor cripple in Lystra, who could use neither foot and had never walked (14: 8–10), and restored the lad Eutychus to life when he had been overcome by sleep during Paul's sermon and fallen from the third storey and been killed (20: 7–12).

(4) *The Poor*. Some of the disciples of Jesus were well-to-do (e.g., Joseph of Arimathea), as were some of those who responded in St. Paul's missions (e.g., Acts 16: 14–15; 17: 12), but the majority were poor. Not many wise, mighty or noble were called (1 Cor. 1: 26–9). Jesus fulfilled Isaiah's prophecy which He read in the Nazareth synagogue (Is. 61: 1–2), preached the good news to the poor (Lk. 4: 18; 7: 22) and promised them the Kingdom of God (6: 20). Our Lord's own mother was a poor woman who brought 'a pair of turtle doves or two young pigeons' for her purification because she could not afford a lamb (2: 22–4; Lev. 12: 6–8). The Saviour Himself was born in a stable, laid in a manger, visited by shepherds, and provided for from the means of ministering women (8: 2–3). The disciples were to give to beggars (6: 29–30), and to sell their possessions and give alms (12: 33; cf. 11: 41 and 19: 8). The rich man giving a dinner party or a banquet should invite not his wealthy friends and neighbours and relatives but 'the poor, the maimed, the lame and the blind' (14: 12–14). Only Luke records these sayings of Jesus, and only Luke includes the parables of Dives and Lazarus (16: 19–31), the Unjust Steward (16: 1–13), and the Rich Fool (12: 13–21), which are all concerned with God and mammon. The three synoptists tell the story

of the Rich Young Ruler. Matthew and Mark say he went away 'sorrowful because he had great possessions'. Luke says he went away exceedingly sorrowful because 'he was *very* rich' (18: 23). In the Acts Luke reveals great interest in the early fellowship of the believers, which led them to have all things common (2: 34 and 44–5; 4: 32–5: 11); speaks of Paul's share with Barnabas in the relief which the church of Antioch sent to the famine-stricken churches of Judea (11: 27–30); and mentions the Church's care for Christian widows (6: 1–6 and 9: 41; cf. Lk. 4: 25; 7: 12; 18: 3).

(5) *The Outcasts.* It was Dante who described Luke as the 'writer of the story of the gentleness of Christ', and in no case is this more apparent than in his record of Jesus' treatment of sinners. It is true that Luke tells of three occasions on which Jesus went in to dine with a Pharisee (7: 36; 11: 37; 14: 1), but he represents Him chiefly as fraternizing with 'publicans and sinners' (15: 1–2). It was when such drew near to hear Him, that He told the three parables of Lost Treasure (the Lost Sheep, the Lost Coin and the Lost Son, 15: 3–32), which are unique in Luke's Gospel.

'Publicans' were universally despised in Palestine. They were tax-collectors or customs officials, directly or indirectly employed by the hated Romans, and they normally had to rely for their livelihood on whatever extra money they could extort from their unfortunate victims. Both politically and morally they were outcasts. But Luke reveals in his Gospel that God loves them. John the Baptist preached to them (3: 12–13). Jesus called one, Levi by name, into the apostolic band, and Levi then made a great feast in his own house to which he invited both Jesus and a large company of his business associates. The Pharisees raised their eyebrows, but Jesus defended His behaviour in 'eating and drinking with publicans and sinners' by His well-known epigram: 'Those who are well have no need of a physician, but those who are sick—I have not come to call the righteous, but sinners to repentance' (5: 27–32). Another publican, an excise official from Jericho, diminutive Zacchæus, received salvation from Jesus, and Jesus went to his house. The criticism of the bystanders on this occasion, and Zacchæus' remarkable promise of restitution, brought from Jesus' lips the saying which only Luke has preserved: 'The Son of man came to seek and to save that which was lost' (19: 1–10). It is also Luke who tells the parable of the Pharisee and the Publican who went into the Temple to pray, with its unexpected conclusion, which must have profoundly shocked His hearers, that the publican 'went down to his house justified rather than the other' (18: 9–14). It is these unwanted sinners who are to be invited into the Kingdom, just as the man who made a great banquet sent his servant to bring in the 'poor, maimed, blind and lame' from the city and to go 'into the highways and hedges and compel people to come in' (14: 15–24). It is not only in the case of publicans that the mercy of Jesus to outcasts is revealed. Luke describes two other incidents, which belong to this Gospel only, which exhibit the grace of God to sinners. The first is the story of the prostitute who came silently behind Him as He reclined at table in the house of Simon the Pharisee. The feet washing which His host had not supplied, she gave Him—with her tears. She also anointed His feet with ointment and covered them with kisses. He did not shrink from her. She had been forgiven. So she loved much (7: 36–50). The other incident took place at the end. Matthew and Mark give us the bare information that two robbers were crucified with Jesus, one on each side of Him, and that they joined in the chorus of abuse which the scribes and elders were hurling at Him. But Luke adds the conversation which took place between the penitent thief and the Saviour. He had some glimmering faith in the kingship of Jesus, and he received the promise: 'To-day shalt thou be with Me in Paradise' (23: 39–43).

(6) *Foreigners.* If Luke shows how the grace of God could reach down to the lowest, he also shows how its broad sweep could gather in all the nations. The ancients were perhaps not altogether fanciful when they saw in the shape of the cross a parable of the breadth and depth and height of the love of God (cf. Eph. 3: 18–19). It is this inclusion of all nations which most clearly distinguishes Luke's presentation of the Gospel. His two-volume history of early Christianity begins in the Temple, but ends near Cæsar's palace. He describes the march of the gospel from Jerusalem, the capital of Jewry, to Rome, the capital of the world. He includes many special incidents in his Gospel to illustrate his theme and to exhibit the universal grace of the Lord. The Acts is a carefully constructed story of how God revealed and began to fulfil His purpose to include the Gentiles in His Church.

THE GOSPEL

After the preface, Luke's Gospel begins in a thoroughly Jewish atmosphere. The scene is set in the Temple at Jerusalem, and the first figure to whom we are introduced is a priest married to one of the daughters of Aaron. The son promised to this pious couple is to keep the ancient Nazarite's vow from his birth, 'will turn many of the sons of Israel to the Lord their God, and will go before Him in the spirit and power of

Elijah' (Lk. 1: 5–17). We are then introduced to another couple, this time living in the north country and belonging to the house of David. The child promised to Mary will be the long-awaited Messiah. He will be given 'the throne of His father David, and He will reign over the house of Jacob for ever' (1: 26–38). Mary goes south to the Judean hills to meet her kinswoman Elizabeth, and during the course of these months the Spirit of the Lord comes upon His servants causing them to prophesy in the sublime words we know as the *Magnificat* (1: 46–55), the *Benedictus* (1: 67–79) and the *Nunc Dimittis* (2: 29–32).

This Jewish atmosphere is not accidental. Luke, who is writing his Gospel for Gentile readers, does not mean to suggest that Christianity is a new religion with no historical roots in the past. This that has come to pass is a fulfilment of God's covenant with Abraham and of His promises through the prophets (1: 54–5, 70, 72–3). 'It is easier for heaven and earth to pass away, than for one tittle of the law to fail' (Lk. 16: 17) and 'all things must be fulfilled which were written in the law of Moses, and in the prophets, and in the psalms concerning Me' (Lk. 24: 44). But the fulfilment is richer than the expectation, and from the throne of David He will be seen to reign over the whole world.

So chapter 2 opens with a reference not to Herod the Great (1: 5) but to the Emperor Augustus (2: 1). The context widens. Luke begins now to be concerned not with the writings of the prophets, but with the decrees of Cæsar, not with priests but with governors, not with Jerusalem and the Temple, but with Rome and 'all the world'. The Holy Babe is born, it is true, in Bethlehem, the city of David, and the angelic announcement is made to simple Jewish shepherds in the fields nearby. But if the Christmas gospel is for 'all the people' (*sc.* of the Jews. 2: 11), the heavenly host promise peace on earth among men with whom God is pleased, and no racial reference is made (2: 14). When the child is brought to the Temple to be presented to the Lord, the aged and godly Simeon is inspired by the Spirit to perceive the fulfilment of Isaiah's prophecies (Is. 42: 6; 49: 6). He recognizes in Jesus the salvation which God had prepared for 'all peoples' and the light which would be both for revelation to the Gentiles and for glory to His people Israel (2: 31–2).

When the silent years have passed, John the Baptist begins his ministry, which Luke places in a world context (3: 1–3) and describes as a preparation for the Messiah's coming when 'all flesh' shall see God's salvation (3: 4–6).

After the Baptism and Temptation of Jesus, whose genealogy he traces back at this point to Adam (3: 21– 4: 13), and a brief reference to Jesus' initial preaching ministry in Galilee (4: 14–15), Luke records the remarkable occasion of His visit to Nazareth (4: 16–30). Some have thought this visit to Nazareth is the same as that which Matthew and Mark describe towards the end of the Galilean ministry. If so, Luke may have purposely altered the sequence of events, in order to make this visit to Nazareth symbolize His rejection by the Jews. Alternatively, it may be a different visit altogether, and certainly there is little verbal similarity between the account of Matthew and Mark and this by Luke. In any case the meaning of the incident to Luke is clear. The context is thoroughly Jewish (in the synagogue, on the sabbath, with a reading from Isaiah), but the mind of Jesus reaches out to the Gentile world. The Lord reminds His listeners that although there were many widows in Israel in the days of Elijah, the prophet was only sent to the Sidonian widow at Zarephath, and that although in the days of Elisha there were many lepers in Israel, none was cleansed except Naaman, the Syrian. The starving widow was fed and the leprous general cured, despite their foreign nationality. This aroused the hostility of His audience. They cast Him out of the city, and led Him to the brow of the hill to throw Him headlong. 'The rejection by Nazareth foreshadows the rejection by the Jewish people and the subsequent universal mission of the Church.'[1]

So during the Galilean ministry Jesus reveals His love for the Gentile stranger. The Roman centurion's servant is healed (7: 1–7), and Luke gives a longer version than Matthew, in which he depreciates himself ('neither thought I myself worthy to come to Thee', 7: 7) and in which it is the Jewish elders themselves who urge his case on Jesus.

If Luke's copy of Mark's Gospel was not mutilated and it included Mark 6: 44–8: 26, the reason why he made this so-called 'great omission' may be that it includes the controversy with the Pharisees over the tradition of the elders (Mk. 7: 1–23) which he may have thought lacking in relevance to his Gentile readers, and the story of the healing of the Syro-Phoenician woman (Mk. 7: 24–30) in which Jesus employs the common Jewish derogatory term for Gentiles and calls them 'dogs'.

The long section of St. Luke's Gospel which stretches from 9: 51–18: 15 is composed exclusively of material not to be found in Mark. It is in fact inserted between the ninth and tenth chapters of Mark and is therefore

[1] *The Gospel According to St. Luke*, by J. M. Creed, p. 66. (Macmillan, 1930.)

sometimes called the 'great interpolation'. It is also
called 'the Lucan Travel Narrative', because it records
some incidents which took place on the borders of
Galilee and Samaria (17: 11), in Samaria and possibly
Peræa (cf. Mk. 10: 1), after Jesus had 'set His face
steadfastly to go to Jerusalem' (9: 51). A special emphasis
is laid in this section on the inclusion of the hated
Samaritans. It is now that Jesus rebuked James and
John, the sons of thunder, for wanting to call down fire
from heaven to consume the Samaritan village which
would not receive them (9: 51-6); that the parable of
the Good Samaritan is told (10: 25-37); and that the
Samaritan leper returns to give thanks for his cleansing
(17: 11-19). It is now also that Jesus sends out the
Seventy. This is recorded by Luke only (10: 1-12). It
was thought from Genesis 10 that there were seventy
nations in the world, and it is probable therefore that
Luke sees in the dispatch of the Twelve an epitome of
the mission to the Jews (cf. Mt. 10: 5-6), and in the
dispatch of the Seventy an epitome of the mission to
the Gentiles. Certainly Jesus saw in the harvest of the
Samaritans the first-fruits of the ingathering of the
nations (Jn. 4: 35-42).

When He reached Jerusalem He predicted its overthrow by the legions of Rome (Lk. 19: 41-4; 21: 20),
and declared that the city would 'be trodden down of
the Gentiles . . . until the times of the Gentiles be fulfilled' (21: 24). Luke had clearly understood this reference to Jerusalem's destruction.

When the end came, and the Lord broke from the
sepulchre on Easter morning, He issued to His disciples
the universal commission. Mark has already mentioned
it (Mk. 13: 10), and Matthew described the occasion on
the Galilean mountain when Jesus sent them forth to

D

make disciples, to baptize and to teach (Mt. 28: 16–20). Luke, at the end of his Gospel, appears to be giving a summary of the Lord's teaching during the forty days. He gives no clear indication of the time or place, but records Jesus' interpretative summary of the Old Testament, namely, that the Christ should suffer **and** rise and that on the basis of that Name there should be preached to all the nations beginning from Jerusalem both repentance (as a demand) and remission (as an offer) (Lk. 24: 44–9).

The gospel ends with a promise of the Spirit's coming to clothe them with power from on high for their task, and then the Lord is parted from them and ascends to heaven.

THE ACTS

It is this ascended Lord who continues through His Spirit in the Acts what He 'began to do and teach' (Acts 1: 1) in the Gospel. The Acts opens in Jerusalem (1: 4), where the Gospel ends (Lk. 24: 52–3). The promise of the Spirit is repeated (Acts 1: 5). Through His power the apostles would bear witness to Christ, and the Kingdom, so far from being restored to Israel, would spread to the uttermost parts of the earth (Acts 1: 6–8).

This great statement of the universal extension of the Kingdom serves to introduce the theme of the Acts. The Day of Pentecost supplies not only its first fulfilment but an illustration of its future history. The chief visible result of the Spirit's arrival was, as Jesus had predicted, that their mouths were opened to speak (2: 4). Moreover, their witness was given in many tongues, so that 'devout men from every nation under heaven' (2: 5) heard 'each in his own native language' (2: 8) 'the mighty works of God' (2: 11). It is true that they were all Jews (2: 5), belonging to the dispersion, but it is clear that their cosmopolitan origins are intended to symbolize the World-Church. The catalogue includes inhabitants of Parthia and Mesopotamia (north), Egypt and Libya (south), Arabia (east), Asia and even Rome (west). Peter's explanation of the phenomenon is that it is a fulfilment of God's promise to pour out His Spirit upon all flesh, not only upon all nations, but upon both sexes ('sons and daughters'), old and young ('young men and old men'), and all ranks of society (even 'men-servants and maidservants'). In fact, as Peter goes on to say, still quoting from Joel *'whosoever* shall call on the name of the Lord shall be saved' (2: 21). In his final appeal he makes it clear that the promise is not only 'to you and your children' but 'to all that are far off' (2: 39), which is a phrase describing the Gentiles. God has kept His covenant with Abraham to bless all the families of the earth through his posterity (3: 25; Gen. 12: 3).

In chapters 3 to 7 the Church in Jerusalem is built up. Nothing can stop the work of God. Satan attacks through the persecution of the authorities (4: 1 *et seqq.*), through the insinuation of evil into the Church itself (5: 1 *et seqq.*) and through the preoccupation of the apostles with material things (6: 1 *et seqq.*). But the Word of God mightily increases. In 2: 41, there are three thousand; in 4: 4 there are five thousand; in 5: 14 there are 'multitudes both of men and women', and in 6: 7 'the number of the disciples multiplied greatly'.

Perhaps the most important feature of these chapters is the defence and martyrdom of Stephen (6: 8–8: 1). His liberal Christian spirit brought upon him the accusation that he had spoken against Moses (6: 11), saying that Jesus would destroy the Temple and change the law (6: 13–14). The charge was serious. Stephen's eloquent and able defence makes it clear what he had in fact been teaching; namely, that the old particularism has been superseded by a new universalism. God is not tied to a building. He dwelt with Abraham in Mesopotamia and Haran and Palestine; with Joseph in Egypt; with Moses in the land of Midian; with the Israelites in the wilderness; with Joshua as he settled the nation in the promised land. True, Solomon built the Temple, but the prophet Isaiah said that God's throne was in heaven and that earth was His footstool. The evidence of the Old Testament is clear, that 'the Most High does not dwell in houses made with hands' (7: 48).

The importance of Stephen's speech and death is threefold. Firstly, theological. His exposition of the theme that God had been present with His people in different places throughout different generations was explosive enough to demolish the whole confined structure of contemporary Judaism. Secondly, personal. Saul of Tarsus was present at his death and consented to it (7: 58–8: 1). He had no doubt heard his inspired speech, seen his shining face (6: 15) and witnessed his Christlike end (7: 54–60). And Saul, whose conversion is related in chapter 9, was to be the great apostle to the Gentiles. Thirdly, geographical. As a result of the persecution which arose over Stephen, Christian believers were 'scattered throughout the region of Judea and Samaria' (8: 1 and 11: 19), and wherever they were they preached (5: 4).

This ushers in *the second phase* of evangelism predicted by Jesus and recorded in Luke, chapters 8–12, namely in Judea and Samaria. The pace quickens, and the tense excitement grows, as the gospel begins to spread far and wide. Philip goes to Samaria and many are both healed and converted (8: 5–13). The Spirit is withheld until the Jerusalem Apostles have confirmed the believers through the laying on of hands, partly no doubt because this is the first case of conversion outside Jerusalem and partly to show that the ancient Samaritan schism is not to be perpetuated (8: 14–24, cf. Jn. 4: 20–4). Philip then preaches Jesus to the Ethiopian eunuch, who was doubtless a Jew, but was influential in an African country, and baptized him (8: 26–40). Next, Saul, the bigoted persecutor of the Christians, is dramatically arrested when on his way to Damascus for further anti-Christian activity, and surrenders to Jesus, who then tells Ananias that the young convert is going to 'carry My Name before the Gentiles' as well as 'the sons of Israel' (9: 15). He at once begins to preach both in Damascus (9: 20) and 'when many days had passed' (9: 23, probably meaning 'after three years' as in Gal. 1: 18) in Jerusalem (9: 26–30). 'So', writes Luke, in one of his periodic summaries, 'the Church throughout all Judea and Galilee and Samaria had peace and was built up and . . . was multiplied' (9: 31).

Peter is then introduced again as the chief actor (9: 32–43), and there is recounted at great length the important story of the conversion of Cornelius (10–11: 18). He was a Roman centurion in the Italian cohort, stationed at Cæsarea. He was a 'godfearer', on the fringe of the synagogue, charitable and pious, but he was a Gentile. He had not been circumcised. God revealed to Peter with unmistakable certainty that it was His purpose to include uncircumcised Gentiles in the Church. First, He gave him the strange vision of the great sheet let down from heaven full of ceremonially unclean animals, reptiles and birds. In his trance Peter heard the voice of the Lord say to him: 'Rise, Peter, kill and eat.' When he objected, the voice said: 'What God has cleansed, you must not call common.' This happened three times. Secondly, when Peter went (in obedience to the vision) with the servants of Cornelius from Joppa to Cæsarea, and preached the gospel to Cornelius and his family, Cornelius evidently believed, and the Holy Spirit fell on him and 'all who heard the word'. Peter concluded that he could not refuse them baptism. Thus by the vision and by the gift of the Spirit, the rightness of the inclusion of the Gentiles was confirmed. Peter was criticized (11: 1–3), but explained that he had only followed the plain teaching of God. 'Who was I that I could withstand God?' (11: 17). 'When they heard this they were silenced. And they glorified God, saying: "Then to the Gentiles also God has granted repentance unto life" ' (11: 18).

When the gospel spread further north to Phœnicia, Cyprus and Antioch, many more Gentiles believed (11: 19–21). Barnabas was sent by the Jerusalem church to investigate, rejoiced when he saw God's grace, and went to Tarsus to fetch Saul (11: 22–5). The disciples were first called 'Christians' in Antioch (11: 26). Secular opposition arose again down south. James, the son of Zebedee, was beheaded by Herod, but Peter, whom Herod imprisoned, was miraculously set free (12: 1–19). Herod was eaten of worms, but the word of God grew and was multiplied (12: 23–4).

THE FIRST MISSIONARY JOURNEY (13–14)

When Barnabas and Saul returned to Antioch after their visit to Jerusalem with relief (11: 27–30; 12: 25), the Holy Spirit made it clear to the Antiochene church that He had a wider ministry for them. So, having been solemnly commended to the grace of God through the

laying on of hands, they set sail with Mark for Cyprus
(13: 1–4). There the proconsul himself was converted
(13: 12). Embarking again, they sailed north to the
Asian coast. On landing at Perga in Pamphylia, John
Mark deserted them and went home, leaving Paul and
Barnabas to climb the steep and dangerous ascent of
3,600 feet to Antioch of Pisidia (13: 13–14). The second
sabbath day, there was such a stir in the whole city that
the Jews were filled with jealousy and began to contradict the apostles (13: 44–5). The result was that Paul
and Barnabas turned to the Gentiles, many of whom
believed (13: 46–9). Leaving Pisidian Antioch, they
walked eastwards to Iconium, where 'a great company
believed, both of Jews and of Greeks' (14: 1), then
south to Lystra and further east to Derbe (14: 8–20).
They then retraced their steps (14: 21–2) appointing
elders in every church (14: 23), and returned to the
Syrian Antioch, from which town this first missionary
journey had begun, and, having gathered the church
together, declared above all how God 'had opened a
door of faith to the Gentiles' (14: 24–8).

While Paul and Barnabas remained in Antioch, some
Jewish Christians came down from Judea and started
teaching that no one could be saved unless he were
circumcised (15: 1). An earnest debate ensued between
Paul and Barnabas on the one hand and these 'Judaizers'
on the other. It was probably at this point that even
Peter withdrew from association with the Gentile
Christians (Gal. 2: 11–14). The disagreement was so
serious that Paul, Barnabas and some of the others were
appointed to go up to Jerusalem to the apostles and
elders to settle the matter. It is likely that on his way
up to Jerusalem Paul wrote his first Epistle, that to the
Galatians, whose theme is that our 'justification', or

acceptance before God, depends not on the law and our works in obedience to it, but on Christ to whom we are united by faith. It is instructive to see how the apostles reached their final decision. Luke gives us a full and illuminating report of the conference. First, Peter gives evidence about the conversion of Cornelius (Acts 15: 7–11). The burden of his speech is that God did not distinguish between 'them' and 'us'. He repeats this contrast three times. 'We' and 'they' received the Holy Spirit (15: 8), were cleansed in heart (15: 9) and 'saved' (15: 10) on the same terms, namely, 'through the grace of the Lord' (15: 10) 'by faith' (15: 9). Next, Paul and Barnabas relate the conversion of the Gentiles on their first missionary journey (15: 12). James, the Lord's brother and the chairman of the conference, then rises and, having referred to the evidence they had just heard, adds, 'and with this the words of the prophets agree'. He proceeds (15: 13–18) to quote from Amos, Jeremiah and Isaiah. The confirmation of experience by Scripture leads him to propose the epoch-making decision that circumcision is not required of converts from heathenism, but that all Christians be required to abstain from idolatrous and impure practices and also (as a policy concession to ensure harmonious table fellowship between Gentile and Jewish Christians), from 'what is strangled and from blood' (15: 19–21). Once the principle had been secured that circumcision was not necessary for Gentile converts, this kind of concession in policy was permitted. The decision marks a turning point in Luke's narrative, as in the history of the Christian Church. The Christian Church emerged from being a Jewish sect to being the universal religion Christ came to found. Thence, the advance of the gospel gathers momentum rapidly.

THE SECOND MISSIONARY JOURNEY

The second missionary journey began at once. Paul
and Silas, armed with the apostolic decrees, revisited
the Galatian churches (15: 36–16: 5), and, being prevented from continuing further south, west or north,
were obliged to go north-west to Troas (16: 6–8). There
Paul had his vision of a Macedonian beckoning him to
'come over into Macedonia and help us'. This vision
could have only one meaning. A discussion with Silas
and Timothy, and with Luke who had joined the missionary party in Troas, convinced them that God was
calling them to preach the gospel in Macedonia (16:
9–10). This was the greatest event in the second missionary journey. They set sail from Troas and landed
on European soil. The prophecy of Jesus was beginning
to be fulfilled. The vanguard of the gospel army was
pushing forward to 'the uttermost parts of the earth'.
Missions were held in Philippi (16: 11–40), Thessalonica
(17: 1–9) and Berœa (17: 16–13). Paul went on alone
to Athens, where he preached his famous sermon on
the Areopagus (17: 10–34), and then to Corinth where,
owing to strong Jewish opposition, he turned decisively
from the Jews to the Gentiles (18: 1–6). He stayed in
Corinth eighteen months (18: 11), and finally sailed
back to Antioch, calling in at Cenchrea and Ephesus
and Cæsarea on the way (18: 18–22).

THE THIRD MISSIONARY JOURNEY

'After spending some time' in Antioch, he set out
again for the mission field, this time on his third journey
(18: 23). He passed through Galatia to Ephesus. There,
after preaching for three months in the synagogue,
pleading with the Jews (19: 8), he withdrew, owing to

their stubbornness, and started an apologetic preaching ministry in the lecture hall of one Tyrannus (19: 9). 'This continued for two years, so that all the residents of Asia heard the word of the Lord, both Jews and Greeks' (19: 10). Paul's missionary farsightedness began now to conjure up a vision of Rome (19: 21). After a tremendous uproar in Ephesus (19: 23–41) Paul left, and, calling on the churches of Macedonia and Greece on the way (20: 1–5), Troas, Miletus (where he addressed the elders of the Ephesian church, 20: 15–38), and other ports, he landed at Cæsarea (21: 1–14) and finally reached Jerusalem (21: 15). In the Temple, where he had gone by agreement with James to disarm the Jewish Christians who suspected him of disloyalty (21: 17–26) Paul was arrested (21: 27–36).

THE JOURNEY TO ROME

This is the beginning of the end. Paul had to endure a tedious series of trials and defences, first before the mob (21: 37–22: 21), then before Claudius Lysias the tribune and the sanhedrin (22: 30–23: 10), and then before Felix the governor and a deputation from Jerusalem (23: 11–24: 27). Two years later (24: 27), he was again tried, this time by Festus (25: 1 *et seqq.*), and he appealed to Cæsar (25: 11–12). After a further trial before Festus, King Agrippa and Queen Bernice (25: 13–26: 32), Paul and some other prisoners were delivered to a centurion of the Augustan cohort, called Julius, and they set sail in a vessel which was bound for the ports along the Asian coast (27: 1–2). Aristarchus was among them. So was Luke himself. It was an exciting voyage, but after many hazards and the shipwreck on the coast of Malta, the company finally arrived and disembarked at Puteoli in the bay of Naples (27: 3–28: 13). Thence they walked along the great Appian Way to Rome. Here Paul, after three days, summoned the local leaders of the Jews and explained his presence among them (28: 17–22). On an appointed day, they came in large numbers to his house where he was guarded by a soldier (28: 16 and 23). As he argued with them from the Scriptures about Jesus and the Kingdom of God, some believed and some disbelieved (28: 23–4). Before letting them go, Paul quoted Isaiah 6: 9–10 against them and added: 'Let it be known to you then that this salvation of God has been sent to the Gentiles; they will listen.'

Luke finishes his book abruptly. He tells us that Paul remained for two whole years in his own hired house, welcoming all who came to him, preaching the Kingdom of God, and teaching about the Lord Jesus Christ, 'quite openly and unhindered' (28: 30–1). Then Luke lays down his pen. His work is finished. Whether he had possibly been writing it during the two years' wait in Rome, and he had no further news to relate, or whether he was writing much later, and some accident, even his own death, prevented him from finishing the work, we do not know. The abrupt end is not inappropriate. Paul is in the capital of the world. He is proclaiming the good news to all who come to him. No man is hindering him. The scene symbolizes the door of opportunity before the Church. The world lies at its feet. The cross surmounts the orb. It is fitting that Luke should finish there, having demonstrated conclusively that the gospel of our Lord Jesus Christ is for men and women, children and adults, rich and poor, sick and healthy, the good and the bad, Gentiles and Jews. 'All flesh shall see the salvation of God.'

Chapter III

THE MESSAGE OF PAUL

I am not ashamed of the gospel of Christ: for it is the power of God unto salvation to every one that believeth, to the Jew first, and also to the Greek.—Romans 1: 16

The just shall live by faith—Romans 1: 17 and Galatians 3: 11, quoted from Habakkuk 2: 4

WE have already seen that Luke was Paul's friend, companion and doctor. He must have derived much of his understanding of Christianity from Paul. Nevertheless, their emphasis is different. They both think of Jesus as the Saviour and write of His salvation (Luke 2: 11; 7: 50; 19: 10; Acts 2: 21; 4: 12 etc.), but whereas Luke stresses the world-wide extent of this salvation, Paul defines what it is and how it may be received. Luke elaborates the universality, and Paul the gratuity, of the gospel. Luke's theme is 'all flesh shall see the salvation of God', while Paul's is 'by grace are ye saved through faith' (Eph. 2: 8).

Paul was born in Tarsus, the principal city of Cilicia (Acts 9: 11; 21: 39; 22: 3). It was a town of considerable commercial importance and possessed a university which ranked in fame with those of Athens and Alexandria. It is highly unlikely that Paul ever studied in the university, but he will have imbibed something of the Greek atmosphere of the city. He spoke and wrote Greek with great fluency, and could quote if necessary from Aratus (Acts 17: 28), Menander (1 Cor. 15: 33) and Epimenides (Tit. 1: 12). He enjoyed Roman citizenship by birth (Acts 22: 28), which was an uncommon distinction in the provinces, and this probably accounts for the fact that he had the Roman name 'Paul' as well as the Hebrew 'Saul' (Acts 13: 9).

Nevertheless, he was a Jew, belonging to the little but loyal tribe of Benjamin (Phil. 3: 5; Rom. 11: 1). Although living in the dispersion, his family had resisted the rising tides of Hellenism, and still cherished the language and customs of their forefathers, so that Paul could describe himself as 'a Hebrew of the Hebrews' (Phil. 3: 5, cf. 2 Cor. 11: 22; Acts 21: 40 and 22: 2). He was 'circumcised on the eighth day' (Phil. 3: 5). His father was a Pharisee, and perhaps his grandfather before him (Acts 23: 6), and he was himself destined to become one. Probably at a very early age he left his home in Tarsus for Jerusalem, there to study in the school of Rabbi Gamaliel (Acts 22: 3), 'the greatest living exponent of Jewish orthodoxy',[1] and the grandson of the famous Hillel. The Pharisees, as distinct from the unpractical Sadducees, 'set themselves to work to make the observance of the law possible for all earnest Jews.[2]' They had reduced the law neatly to a catalogue of 248 commandments and 365 prohibitions. Young Saul of Tarsus threw himself eagerly into the task of memorizing and observing these statutes and traditions. He was 'educated according to the strict manner of the law of our fathers', was 'zealous for God' (Acts 22: 3; 26:5) and 'as to righteousness under the law blameless' (Phil. 3: 6). Indeed, he claimed when writing to the

[1] *St. Paul: a Christian Study of His Life and Letters*, by A. R. Whitham, p. 7. (Rivingtons, 1929.)
[2] *The Life of St. Paul, the Man and the Apostle*, by F. J. Foakes-Jackson, p. 79. (Jonathan Cape, 1933.)

Galatian churches that he outstripped his contemporaries in what he calls 'Judaism', 'so extremely zealous was I for the traditions of my fathers' (Gal. 1: 13–14). The final proof of his earnest passion for the faith of his fathers was his savage and bigoted persecution of the Christian Church (Acts 22: 4–5; 24: 9–11; Gal. 1: 13; Phil. 3: 6; 1 Tim. 1: 13).

His conversion on the road to Damascus was sudden and dramatic, but it was not altogether unprepared. Various attempts have been made to reconstruct the events and experiences which led to Saul's conversion, and certain predisposing factors, in God's providence, may be detected. The first is his presence on the occasion of Stephen's speech and martyrdom (Acts 7: 58–8: 1). It cannot have been an accident that Luke thus introduces his readers to the figure who is to play the chief part in the second volume of his book. Stephen's able, spiritual exposition of the story of the patriarchs, the beauty of his face as it shone like an angel's, and his self-control in praying, like his Master, for his tormentors, cannot have failed to leave some kind of impression on the mind of the 'young man named Saul' at whose feet the enraged mob laid their garments. Secondly, there was some kind of moral and spiritual struggle disturbing his inner peace. The very vehemence of his attack on the Christians betrays a deep-seated uneasiness. He was 'kicking against the goads' (Acts 26: 14) like a young, untamed ox. Many writers have suggested that the autobiographical references in Romans 7 give us the clue we are seeking. In graphic terms he describes a personal experience, if not 'an experience of his inner life in childhood'[1] then at least a pre-conversion experience.

---

[1] *Paul: a Study in Social and Religious History*, by Adolf Deissmann, p. 91.(Hodder & Stoughton, 1911.)

'I was once alive apart from the law. Then the commandment came; sin revived; and I died' (Rom. 7: 9). To which commandment is he referring? To the tenth (7: 7): 'I should not have known what it is to covet if the law had not said: "You shall not covet".' This tenth commandment is the one which lifts the decalogue from a mere code of outward laws to an inward moral standard. Coveting belongs to thoughts and motives, not to deeds and words. One day, then, Saul the Pharisee realized that he was not blameless as touching the righteousness of the law. He had been guilty of wrong thoughts and desires. He had coveted. He awoke to the fact that he was a sinner. He was spiritually 'dead' (7: 8–11), estranged from God, the source of life. Moreover, he was not his own master. He had the will to do good, but not the power (7: 13–20). He was a slave.

Thirdly, his mind must have been full of doubts and questionings. He probably never saw Jesus in the flesh, but he must have heard much about Him. He knew He had been hailed as the Messiah. He also knew that He had ended His days on a cross. This settled the question for Saul. The idea of a crucified Messiah was monstrous. It was not just that the cross was the Romans' 'gallows'. It was also the Jews' 'tree', and the law stated quite clearly, 'cursed is every one that hangeth on a tree' (Deut. 21: 23). It was utterly impossible to credit the rumour that He had risen from the dead, if He ended His life as a malefactor under the divine curse.

It was this man who was walking at noon along the road from Jerusalem to Damascus. Personally attracted, morally and spiritually dissatisfied, intellectually perplexed, he was stifling his warring thoughts and emotions with fresh persecuting zeal. Suddenly a brilliant light flashed from heaven and blinded him, an unseen hand knocked him to the ground and 'laid hold of' him (Phil. 3: 12), a voice called him by name, and he saw Jesus. There can be no doubt that it was a true objective vision of the risen Christ. It was no hallucination. Paul is quite clear in the matter. He concludes his catalogue of the resurrection appearances (still using the same Greek word) by a reference to himself: 'and last of all, as to one untimely born, He appeared also to me' (1 Cor. 15: 8, cf. 1 Cor. 9: 1).

This personal encounter with the risen Jesus Christ resolved all his conflicts. The Crucified was the Messiah after all. Men had hanged Him on a tree, but God had raised Him from the dead. There must be some other explanation of the cross and its curse. The law pronounced Him accursed, it is true, but God had contradicted the law by raising Him. He was vindicated. Therefore the law must be abrogated. Besides this, he found himself now in relationship to God. He had that 'righteousness' which involves relationship with God and for which he had so long striven in vain. He had not achieved it by his own efforts. Jesus Christ had given it him. It was a free gift (Rom. 5: 17). He had simply surrendered and believed. These great convictions invaded his mind as the light shone from heaven. That revelation of the risen Jesus demonstrated at one and the same time that He was the Christ, that the law was superseded and that eternal life was a gift received by faith. He at once began to preach Jesus in His person as 'the Christ' and 'the Son of God' (Acts 9: 20, 22), and in His work as 'the Saviour' (Acts 13: 23, 26). His experience of the grace of God coloured his theological emphasis. By one act of sovereign grace Jesus Christ had made him a Christian and an apostle (1 Tim. 1: 12–16; Gal. 1: 15–16). His own personal salvation and his special 'gospel' for the Gentiles had both come 'through the revelation of Jesus Christ' (Gal. 1: 11–12, 16). Grace is 'the free and unmerited favour of God'.[1] It is Paul's word to describe the loving, undeserved initiative of God in giving Christ to die, raising Him from the dead and revealing Him to sinners. His whole message became 'the word of His grace' (Acts 14: 3) and 'the good news of the grace of God' (Acts 20: 24). 'The grace of God has appeared for the salvation of all men' (Tit. 2: 11). It is supremely manifested in the provision and offer of salvation. By 'salvation' Paul is using a word with the broadest possible concept. It includes the past, the present and the future. It describes God's liberation of man from all the ravages of sin in the conscience, the mind, the heart, the will and the body; in his relation to God, the world and himself. To use Paul's own words, it comprises the believer's justification (his acceptance before God), sanctification (his growth in holiness), edification (his life in the Church) and glorification (his perfection in the eternal glory). Or more simply, it makes him a son and a saint, a brother and an heir. Such is the grace of Christ received by faith. The only function of faith is to respond to grace. Faith takes what grace offers.

It is a very difficult task to compose a concise and accurate summary of Paul's theology. Thirteen of the New Testament epistles (excluding the Epistle to the Hebrews) are traditionally assigned to him, and, although the Pauline authorship of the Pastoral Epistles to Timothy and Titus is disputed by many, we shall be content in this chapter to assume that he wrote them all. Before considering their contents it may be helpful to group them according to their date and

[1] *Oxford Dictionary.*

subject matter. The polemical Epistle to the Galatians is probably the first, written at the conclusion of the first missionary journey, setting Christ forth as the great Liberator. Next come 'the primer-epistles',[1] the first and second letters to the Thessalonians, written during the second missionary journey, just after his first visit to Thessalonica. These exhibit Christ supremely as the coming Judge. The Epistles to the Romans and the Corinthians (1 and 2), to which some add the Epistle to the Galatians because of the similarity of the subject matter, belong to the third group, and were written during the third missionary journey. They describe the work of Christ, the Saviour. The fourth group consists of the Prison Epistles (those to the Philippians, the Ephesians, the Colossians, and to Philemon), written during Paul's first detention in Rome, manifesting Christ as the Lord of both universe and Church. The fifth and last group includes the Pastoral Epistles (those to Timothy and Titus), written before and during Paul's second and final Roman imprisonment, revealing Christ as the Administrator of His Church on earth. We might tabulate this information thus:

Approx. Dates	Period	Group	Epistles	Presentation of Christ
1. 48–50	End of 1st Missionary Journey	Polemical	Galatians	The Liberator
2. 51–53	During 2nd Missionary Journey	Primer	1 and 2 Thessalonians	The Judge
3. 54–58	During 3rd Missionary Journey	Major	1 and 2 Corinthians Romans	The Saviour

[1] *St. Paul's Conception of Christianity*, by A. B. Bruce. (T. & T. Clark, 1894.)

Approx. Dates	*Period*	*Group*	*Epistles*	*Presentation of Christ*
4. 61–63	During 1st Imprisonment	Prison	Colossians Philemon Ephesians Philippians	The Lord
5. 64–68	During release and subsequent 2nd Imprisonment	Pastoral	1 Timothy Titus 2 Timothy	The Administrator[1]

Many scholars have tried to trace a development of thought in these groups of Paul's epistles, and it is principally for this reason that they have wanted to add Galatians to the third group. Development there undoubtedly was, but we must beware both of classifying Paul's thought too tidily according to date and of supposing that in his later epistles he contradicted the teaching of his earlier days. The Holy Spirit clearly revealed more truth to him as the years passed, but not in such a way as to make him abandon or modify His earlier revelation.

His emphasis throughout is on salvation by grace, through faith. We must now examine this theme in its four variations, mentioned earlier.

(1) JUSTIFICATION

The apostle begins his great Christian manifesto to the Romans by proving all men to be sinners—whether they are Gentiles, who know something of God through the creation (Rom. 1: 18–2: 11) and the light of nature and conscience (2: 12–16), or Jews, who 'know His will' because they are 'instructed in the law' (2: 17–3: 8).

---

[1] It must be added that the precise order in which St. Paul wrote his epistles is still disputed by scholars.

Therefore, as various Psalms make so plain, 'none is righteous, no, not one' (3: 9–18). In fact, every mouth is stopped, and the whole world is guilty before God (3: 19–20). It is this fact of universal human sin and guilt which poses the fundamental question which Bildad the Shuhite had asked Job years before, 'how can man be just before God?' (Job 25: 4).

The Old Testament answer is definite. 'In Thy sight shall no man living be justified' (Ps. 143: 2). God had made it plain in the Law. Human magistrates were commanded to 'justify the righteous and condemn the wicked' (Deut. 25: 1). It was written clearly in the Proverbs (17: 15) that he who condemns the righteous and he who justifies the wicked are both an abomination unto the Lord. How then could God do what He tells man not to do? He says Himself: 'I will by no means justify the wicked' (Ex. 23: 7). And yet Paul startles his readers by describing God (Rom. 4: 5) as He 'who justifies the ungodly'. How can this be?

The most illuminating phrase in Paul's epistles to explain this mystery is in Galatians 2: 17, where he speaks of Christian believers as being 'justified *in Christ*' (literally). This expression to be 'in Christ', which is very common in Paul's letters, means to be united to Christ, to be joined inseparably to Christ, so as to lose one's independence in the sight of God. It is then that one is 'justified' or pronounced righteous.

What virtue, then, is there in Christ that a sinner, by union with Him, may be justified? This brings us to the heart of Paul's argument. He returns to it again and again in his epistles, but perhaps the clearest and most striking example is to be found in 2 Corinthians 5: 21: 'For our sake He made Him to be sin who knew no sin [that is, Christ], so that we might become the righteousness of God in Him.' He became what we are, that we might become what He is. He who was sinless was made sin on the cross, so that we who are unrighteous might become God's righteousness. Then he adds at the end of the sentence the two most important words of all, 'in Him'. He was 'made sin' on the cross. But we do not 'become God's righteousness' until we are individually united to Christ.

This is how Paul was able to solve his pre-conversion dilemma about a crucified Messiah. Since He was hanged on a tree, the law declared Him accursed. But the Resurrection pronounced Him vindicated. How could these apparently contradictory facts be reconciled? Only by supposing the curse He bore was ours. We are under the law's curse by reason of our transgressions. 'Cursed is every one who continueth not in all things which are written in the book of the law to do them' (Gal. 3: 10, quoting Deut. 27: 26). But 'Christ hath redeemed us from the curse of the law, having become a curse for us, for it is written: "Cursed is every one who hangeth on a tree" ' (Gal. 3: 13). He bore our sin and our curse, that we might be set free from them. But what is this curse which the law meets out to sin? It is death. 'The wages of sin is death' (Rom. 6: 23). Spiritual death is that estrangement from God which sin inevitably causes. Death is the only exit to the prison house of sin. 'He who has died has been justified from his sin' (Rom. 6: 7, literally). This death Christ died for us. He died our death. If, then, we are united to Christ, it is as true to say: 'I died in Christ' as it is to say: 'He died for me'. Since Christ died my death and I am in Him, God sees me as if I had died myself. Having died and risen with Christ, the law's demands are met, and I am set free. 'I have been crucified with Christ; it is no longer I who

live but Christ who lives in me' (Gal. 2: 20). 'The love
of Christ constrains us, because we are convinced that
one has died for all; therefore all have died. And He
died for all, that those who live might live no longer
for themselves but for Him who died for them and was
raised' (2 Cor. 5: 15). 'The death He died He died to
sin, once for all, but the life He lives He lives to God.
So you also must consider yourselves dead to sin and
alive to God in Christ Jesus' (Rom. 6: 10–11).

Of this saving union with Christ in His death and
resurrection, baptism is the sign or 'sacrament' (Rom.
6: 3–5; Gal. 3: 26–7; Col. 2: 12). But baptism is not the
means of union. This is clear from a comparison between baptism and circumcision. Baptism is the sign of
entry into the New Covenant, as circumcision was the
sign of entry into the Old Covenant. Now circumcision
is defined by Paul as 'a sign or seal of the righteousness
which he (*sc.* Abraham) had *by faith* while he was still
uncircumcised' (Rom. 4: 11). First Abraham received
justification by faith. Then he received circumcision as
a sign. It is by faith that we are joined to Christ and so
justified (Rom. 3: 22–6), and of this faith Abraham and
David are the best Old Testament examples (Rom. 4;
Gal. 3: 6–9).

So the circle is complete. God can be just and the
justifier of sinners only because He is 'just and the
justifier of him *who believes in Jesus*' (Rom. 3: 26), since
by faith we are united to Christ in His death and
resurrection.

Paul never grows tired of drawing the contrast between human self-righteousness and divine righteousness (Gal. 2: 16; Eph. 2: 8–10; Tit. 3: 4–7; Rom. 10: 3).
It is a contrast born of his own experience. At one time
he had had confidence in himself (Phil. 3: 3–6), but now

he had gained Christ (3: 7–8) who is God's righteousness (cf. 1 Cor. 1: 30). Now his delight was to 'be found in Christ, not having a righteousness of my own, based on law, but that which is through faith in Christ, the righteousness from God that depends on faith' (Phil. 3: 9). It was their self-righteousness which made the cross a stumbling-block to the Jews (1 Cor. 1: 23). So Paul even declares in Galatians 2: 21, that if justification could be obtained through the Law, Christ died to no purpose, for if we could achieve salvation by our own efforts, Christ need not have come to die for our sins. Further, in his Epistle to the Galatians he paints a vivid contrast between Moses and Jesus. Moses administers law, Jesus exhibits grace. Moses says 'work'; Jesus says 'believe'. Moses says that salvation is 'through the works of the law'; Jesus says it is 'in Me, by grace through faith'. Moses holds us in bondage as slaves; Jesus sets us free and makes us sons. This contrast is drawn out in Galatians 3: 23–4: 11 (cf. Acts 13: 38–9). It is the same contrast which Jesus drew in His parable of the Pharisee and the Publican (Lk. 18: 9–14); which was rediscovered at the Reformation; and which was incorporated in our Article 11 *Of Justification*: 'We are accounted righteous before God only for the merit of our Lord and Saviour Jesus Christ through faith, and not for our own works or deservings. Wherefore, that we are justified by faith only is a very wholesome doctrine and very full of comfort . . .'. There is perhaps no message which needs more to be recovered and proclaimed in our generation.

The doctrine is much maligned because it is much misunderstood. Paul was sensitive to his opponent's criticisms and answers three questions which no doubt were addressed to him, the third of which will introduce our second section.

(i) If salvation is by grace through faith in Christ, what then is the purpose of the law? He reverts to this theme in Romans 3: 20, 31; 7: 7–14, and Galatians 3: 19–29. The law is our 'pedagogue' or 'custodian' until Christ came. The *Paidagogos* in Greek households was the disciplinarian, responsible for supervising the boy while a minor, until the day set by his father for the attainment of his majority as a son. So the law, by revealing and even provoking our sin, kept us under restraint until Christ came as the Saviour we needed. 'Christ is the end of the law, that every one who has faith may be justified' (Rom. 10: 4).

(ii) If salvation is by grace through faith, 'what advantage has the Jew?' (Rom. 3: 1–8). Is not the Gentile just as favoured? Paul's answer is manifold. The Jews had the privilege of being entrusted with God's oracles. 'To them belong the sonship, the glory, the covenants, the giving of the law, the worship, and the promises; to them belong the patriarchs, and of their race, according to the flesh, is the Christ' (Rom. 9: 4–5). Further, God has not cast off His people, but one day, when 'the full number of the Gentiles' has come in, 'all Israel will be saved' (Rom. 9–11). Besides, salvation in Christ is a fulfilment of God's promise made ages ago to Abraham (Gal. 3: 14). Christ is 'the hope of Israel' (Acts 26: 6–7; 28: 20). The Church of Christ is the Israel of God, and Christ's own people are Abraham's offspring (Gal. 3: 29; 6: 16). All that has happened is 'according to the Scriptures' (Rom. 3: 21; 1 Cor. 15: 3, etc.).

(iii) If salvation is by grace through faith, can we sin as we please? If God's forgiveness issues from His free and undeserved love, can we go on sinning that He may go on forgiving? 'Shall we continue in sin, that grace may abound?' (Rom. 6: 1). The so-called 'antinomians' who denied the necessity of holiness were as dangerous in their opposition to the truth as the Judaizers who denied that acceptance before God depends on grace through faith. Both were 'enemies of the cross of Christ' (Phil. 3: 19) since

> *He died that we might be forgiven,*
> *He died to make us good.*

This third objection to Paul's doctrine of justification by faith, leads us to consider the second stage in our salvation.

(2) SANCTIFICATION

Justification is a legal pronouncement which is instantaneous. As soon as any sinner turns from his sin and commits himself in absolute trust to Jesus Christ who died for him and rose again, God pronounces him righteous. He is 'accepted in the Beloved' (Eph. 1: 6), or 'justified in Christ' (Gal. 2: 17). Sanctification is, however, a process by which the sinner is gradually transformed into the image of Christ (2 Cor. 3: 18). The two are inseparably connected. Deliberate continuance in sin is therefore a sheer impossibility. The believer has been united to Christ in His Resurrection as well as in His death. He has died in Christ to sin, but he has risen with Christ to newness of life (Rom. 6: 1–11; 2 Cor. 5: 14–15; Col. 2: 20–3: 4). If God has made Christ 'our justification', He has also made Him 'our sanctification' (1 Cor. 1: 30). If we are in Christ for acceptance, we are in Christ for holiness also. We are indeed 'saved', but we must 'work out our own salvation' in daily behaviour, 'with fear and trembling' (Phil. 2: 12–13).

So several of Paul's epistles can be clearly divided

into two halves, the first doctrinal, the second ethical; the first relating to the Christian faith, and the second to the Christian life (cf. Rom. 1–11 and 12–16; Gal. 1–4 and 5–6; Eph. 1–3 and 4–6; Col. 1–2 and 3–4). So, too, he prays earnestly for his converts that they may be filled with truth and love, with righteousness and patience, with joy and thankfulness (see especially Eph. 1: 15–23; 3: 14–19; Phil. 1: 3–11; Col. 1: 9–14). His epistles refer often to the Christian's private life in the home. He tells husbands to love their wives and wives to be submissive to their husbands; children to obey their parents and parents to discipline their children; slaves to serve their masters and masters to be fair to their slaves (Eph. 5: 22–6: 9; Col. 3: 18–4: 1). He tells citizens to respect authority and to pay their taxes (Rom. 13: 1–7). He has some very practical and outspoken words to say about telling lies, losing one's temper, stealing, using bad language and being cantankerous (Eph. 4: 25–5: 2); about impurity of deed and word (Eph. 5: 3–14); about wasting time and getting drunk; about being cheerful, appreciative and humble (Eph. 5: 15–21). He urges on his Philippian friends the Christian virtues of humility and unselfishness (Phil. 2: 1–11); of joy, prayer, peace and contentment (4: 4–13). It is a Christian duty, he tells the Thessalonians, to work for your living and not be idle (1 Thess. 4: 9–12; 2 Thess. 3: 6–13). He is quite clear that the Christian life is a life of moral purity (1 Cor. 5; 6: 9–11; 1 Thess. 4: 1–8). Above all, Christians are not to seek revenge (Rom. 12: 14–21) but to love each other, and all men, for love is the fulfilling of the law (Rom. 13: 8–10; Gal. 5: 13–15).

Such a life of holiness is no more the product of human achievement than is the state of acceptance. Sanctification is as much by grace as is justification. The

Christian soldier will need to take to himself the whole panoply of God if he hopes to withstand the onslaughts of the evil one. It is only 'in the Lord and in the power of His might' that we can be strong (Eph. 6: 10–20). Our enemy, however, is not only 'principalities and powers . . . in heavenly places' (6: 12). It is also 'the flesh' within. This is Paul's word for the lower nature, the self-centredness which is original sin, the inner tendency to wrong. It is the flesh which weakens the law (Rom. 8: 3), because it renders one incapable of obeying the law. Consequently, the law by itself is as helpless to sanctify us as it is to justify us. Again, we need the grace of Jesus not the law of Moses. This time, however, His grace is revealed not in His death but in His gift of the Spirit, through whose indwelling power holiness becomes a possibility. By the same act of faith the sinner is justified (Gal. 2: 16) and receives the Spirit (3: 2). Holiness is a matter not of struggling to obey an external law but of bearing fruit from within. The outworkings of the flesh are obvious, and include immorality, lovelessness, and intemperance. The full catalogue is grim indeed (Gal. 5: 19–21). But 'the fruit of the Spirit' (His natural produce) is the ninefold harvest of love, joy and peace, patience, kindness and goodness, faithfulness, gentleness and self-control (5: 22–3). How may we ensure that our lives manifest the Spirit's fruit and not the flesh's works? By 'crucifying the flesh' (5: 24), resolutely and ruthlessly rejecting its claims to dominate, and by 'walking in the Spirit' (5: 16), living each moment under His control. Then we shall 'not gratify the desires of the flesh' (5: 16). Only so, namely by 'walking according to the Spirit' can we fulfil the just requirements of the law (Rom. 8: 4; and see Rom. 7: 13–8: 9). Christians are in fact of two kinds, 'carnal' (dominated by the flesh) and 'spiritual' (dominated by the Spirit). They are no longer 'natural', because they are indwelt by Him, whose presence is the distinguishing characteristic of the Christian (1 Cor. 2: 14–3: 4; Rom. 8: 9; cf. Jude 19). They possess Him but they may not be possessed by Him. The 'spiritual' Christian both understands and obeys God's will, for the Holy Spirit illumines his mind (1 Cor. 2: 6–3: 2) as well as sanctifies his life (1 Cor. 3: 3–4).

One other part of the apostle's teaching on the subject of sanctification must be mentioned. It concerns incentives. He seldom makes an exhortation to holiness without adding a motive. Sometimes, it is the example of Christ. We are to humble ourselves, as Christ emptied Himself (Phil. 2: 5–7), to 'walk in love as Christ loved us and gave Himself up for us' (Eph. 5: 2) and to 'welcome one another as Christ has welcomed us' (Rom. 15: 7). Sometimes, it is the presence of Christ which is to be our inspiration. We are to submit to one another and bring holiness to perfection 'in the fear of Christ' (Eph. 5: 21; 2 Cor. 7: 1), that is with loving dread of grieving Him in whose presence we live. More often, it is a consideration of who we are and what we have become by God's grace, which will keep us holy. We have died and risen with Christ; therefore we must reckon ourselves to be so (Rom. 6: 1–11), 'mortifying our earthly members' and 'setting our affections on things above' (Col. 2: 20–3: 7). We have received the Spirit; therefore we must walk by Him (Gal. 5: 25). We have put off the old man and put on the new; therefore we must put off anger and lying, and put on love (Col. 3: 8–14). Our bodies are members of Christ, indwelt by the Spirit, and will be raised by the Father; therefore we must glorify God in them since they are His (1 Cor.

6: 12–20). We are God's children; therefore we must cleanse ourselves (2 Cor. 6: 14–7: 1). The fourth incentive to holiness anticipates the last stage of our salvation. It is the Christian hope. We are to live this life in the light of the next. Paul was always working and praying towards 'that day' when the Lord Jesus would appear, and he longed that his converts should be preserved blameless until His coming (cf. 1 Cor. 1: 7–8; 1 Thess. 5: 23; 3: 11–13; 2: 18, etc.). The day would come like a burglar, and God's people must 'cast off the works of darkness' and 'put on the armour of light' in order to be ready (Rom. 13: 11–14; 1 Thess. 5: 1–11).

(3) EDIFICATION

It must not be thought that salvation as Paul describes it is a purely personal affair between the individual soul and God. 'Edification' is the word Paul uses for the building up of the Church, and Christian fellowship is as natural and inevitable a consequence of justification as is sanctification. This can be easily demonstrated by taking his three commonest links.

Firstly, there is the link between 'faith' and 'love'. Not only are these two Christian virtues two of the trilogy of 1 Corinthians 13, but they recur together again and again. He speaks of the Ephesians' and Colossians' 'faith in the Lord Jesus and love toward all the saints' (Eph. 1: 15; Col. 1: 4). He gives thanks for the Thessalonians' 'work of faith and labour of love', and declares to the Galatians that what really matters is neither circumcision nor uncircumcision but 'faith which worketh by love' (Gal. 5: 6). We cannot put our trust in Christ without loving our fellows, for by faith we receive the Spirit (Gal. 3: 2), and the first-fruit of the Spirit is love (Gal. 5: 22).

Secondly, there is the link between sons and brothers, for if we are sons of God, we are brothers one of another. Once again, it is faith which is the great leveller. When, through faith, we are in Christ, we are all of us sons of God (Gal. 3: 26). Therefore, in Christ we are all of us 'one man' (Gal. 3: 28). God no longer sees our human distinctions of race or rank or sex. He only sees Christ (*ibid.*). 'Brother' is therefore one of the commonest words employed by the apostle to describe the Christian. He never uses it idly. Indeed, he derives much practical instruction for life in the fellowship from the fact of the brotherhood. It is inconceivable, he writes to the Corinthians, that brother should go to law against brother, and that before unbelievers (1 Cor. 6: 6). It is equally outrageous that an instructed Christian should so enjoy his Christian liberty as to wound the conscience of a weaker 'brother for whom Christ died' (1 Cor. 8: 11, cf. Rom. 14–15 and 1 Cor. 8). Again, the offering which Paul organized from the churches of Macedonia and Achaia for the church of Jerusalem (1 Cor. 16: 1–4; 2 Cor. 8–9) was an expression of their brotherhood of burden bearing (Gal. 6: 1–10). Paul loves to dwell on Christ's abolition of all social and racial distinctions. He sends the converted runaway slave, Onesimus, back to Colosse, to his former master Philemon, and gives the latter the staggering instruction that he is to receive the slave as 'a beloved brother' (Philem. 16). He elaborates the fact that through the cross Christ 'has broken down the dividing wall of hostility' between Jew and Gentile, and has reconciled each to the other and both to God (Eph. 2: 11–18). Jews and Gentiles are now fellow-citizens in the Kingdom and fellow-members of the household. This is 'the mystery', the secret concealed through previous generations but now revealed specially to Paul (Eph. 2: 19–3: 6; Col. 1: 26). There is no distinction between Jew and Gentile. They have the same need (Rom. 3: 22–30); they have received the same offer (Rom. 10: 12). The gospel is 'the power of God unto salvation—to everyone that believeth, to the Jew first, but also to the Greek' (Rom. 1: 16).

The third link is between the Spirit and the Body. We have already seen that the Spirit is received by the hearing of faith (Gal. 3: 2). He indwells the heart of every son of God (Gal. 4: 6). But the Spirit is one and undivided. Therefore the Church is one and undivided. 'There is one Body and one Spirit' (Eph. 4: 4, cf. 1 Cor. 12: 13). Indeed, there is one Body because there is one Spirit. 'Where the Spirit is, there is the Church' (Irenaeus). The unity of the Church is not to be created. It is to be 'preserved in the bond of peace', for it already exists. It is 'the unity of the Spirit' (Eph. 4: 3) or 'the fellowship of the Spirit' (Phil. 2: 1; 2 Cor. 13: 14). This fellowship or 'koinonia' was a common participation in all the grace of God (Phil. 1: 7). Of this 'communion' the Lord's Supper is the symbol (1 Cor. 10: 16–17; 11: 17–34), for in it God assures us that 'we are very members incorporate in the mystical Body of His Son, which is the blessed company of all faithful people.'

The Church, then, is the Body of Christ. Christ is Head of the Church, as He is Head of the universe (Eph. 1: 20–3; Col. 1: 15–19). The Body derives its life from the Head (Col. 2: 19), and God has made provision for its growth. The Holy Spirit distributes His 'spiritual gifts' to each for the common good of all. Not all have the same gift or gifts. As in the human body there is one body but many members, each with its different function, so in the Body of Christ each

Christian has his particular gift or gifts. These gifts are spiritual aptitudes which fit us for special offices. The full lists are in Ephesians 4: 11–16 and 1 Corinthians 12 (cf. Rom. 12: 3–8). In both passages, the purpose of the gifts is made clear. It is the 'edification', or building up, of Christ's Body to its final completion.

Then there is the settled ministry. Paul ordained elders in the churches in his missionary journeys (Acts 14: 23). In the Pastoral Epistles he gives instructions to Timothy and Titus, the leaders of the churches respectively of Ephesus and Crete, about the selection and appointment of presbyter-bishops (1 Tim. 3: 1–7 and Tit. 1: 5–9) and deacons (1 Tim. 3: 8–13). All such ministers are only 'agents' through whom Christ works (1 Cor. 3: 5–4), but they are to be 'esteemed very highly for their work's sake' (1 Thess. 5: 12–13). Paul gives a good deal more practical advice in the Pastoral Epistles about the internal administration of the church, urging Timothy and Titus to maintain the faith, organize public prayer and Scripture reading, care for the widows, etc., just as in 1 Corinthians he writes of the veiling of women in public worship (11: 2–16), and of the need to regulate the exercise of the gift of tongues (14). All spiritual gifts are to be coveted (12: 31), but the yet more excellent way, by which the Church is chiefly 'edified', is love (1 Cor. 13; Eph. 4: 15–16).

(4) GLORIFICATION

The Christian is not only a 'son' and a 'brother' but thereby also 'an heir of God and joint-heir with Christ' (Rom. 8: 17; Gal. 4: 7). He has not yet entered into his full inheritance. He has, however, received the 'first-fruits' of it, that is, the Holy Spirit Himself (Rom. 8:

23). Changing the metaphor from an agricultural to a commercial one, Paul also calls the Spirit 'the earnest', that is, in modern terms, the 'first instalment', of our inheritance (2 Cor. 1: 22; 5: 5; Eph. 1: 14). His presence in our hearts is God's seal, branding us for His own, and guaranteeing to us our possession of the full and final glory to come.

It will, therefore, be seen that the believer's glorification issues as naturally and surely from his justification as do both his sanctification and his edification. It is the last phase in the outworking of the grace of God. We have seen that when the believer is in Christ, he is justified. 'There is therefore now no condemnation to them that are in Christ Jesus' (Rom. 8: 1). 'Who shall bring any charge against God's elect? It is God who justifies; who is to condemn? It is Christ Jesus who died, yes rather, who was raised from the dead, who is at the right hand of God, who indeed intercedes for us' (Rom. 8: 33–4). Paul is confident of the believer's eternal security, only because he is confident in God's unchanging grace. 'Whom He foreknew, He predestined . . .; whom He predestined, He called; whom He called, He justified; whom He justified, He also glorified' (Rom. 8: 29–30). This chain of divine grace cannot be broken at any of its links. 'Justified by His grace' we become 'heirs in hope of eternal life' (Tit. 3: 7). The sinner is saved 'through faith' but also 'in hope' (Rom. 8: 24). He is 'justified by faith' and so 'rejoices in hope of the glory of God' (Rom. 5: 1–2). Faith looks back to the cross of Christ; hope looks on to His coming and the final glory. Of what does this glorification consist? What is this Christian' hope'? It is sure and steadfast. The very word admits of no uncertainty. It is the joyful and confident expectation of God's final triumph. 'Christ in

F

you' is the 'hope of glory' (Col. 1: 27). His indwelling
presence is the pledge of the future bliss. But what
exactly is the object of the Christian's hope? What
is the coming 'glory'? Paul distinguishes three
elements.

The first is the return of Christ. It is described now
as His 'epiphany' (e.g., 2 Tim. 4: 8), now as His
'presence' (e.g., 2 Thess. 2: 1), now as His 'unveiling'
(e.g., 1 Cor. 1: 7), now as His 'appearing' (Col. 3: 4).
'The Lord Himself shall descend from heaven with a
shout, with the archangel's call, and with the sound of
the trumpet of God' (1 Thess. 4: 16). This 'day of the
Lord' will come 'like a burglar in the night' (1 Thess. 5:
2). But it will not be unheralded. As Jesus Himself had
taught, there would be signs warning of His coming.
It appears that the Thessalonians had become so fas-
cinated by the idea of the Lord's imminent return, that
many of them had started playing truant from work.
Paul writes to them that they must continue to earn
their living (1 Thess. 4: 11–12; 2 Thess. 3: 6–13), and
warns them that the day of the Lord will not come
'unless the rebellion comes first and the man of lawlessness is revealed' (2 Thess. 2: 1–12). Already the spirit
of lawlessness is at work secretly (2: 7), but it is being
held in check. Probably 'what restrains' and 'he who
restrains' is the maintenance of law and order represented
by the person of the Emperor. But the day will come
when lawlessness will break out openly and will be
embodied in a 'man of lawlessness', who is probably to
be identified with the Antichrist. Only then will Christ
come and destroy him (2: 8). Some scholars have sought
to show that Paul modified his ideas with the passage
of years, and no longer expected to be alive at Christ's
return. This theory is difficult to substantiate. In

1 Thessalonians he is expecting to survive, for he uses the phrase 'we who are alive, who are left until the coming of the Lord' (4: 15). Even in 1 Corinthians he says, 'we shall not all sleep, but we shall all be changed' (15: 51). In Philippians, one of the Prison Epistles, written later still, he says he does not expect to die yet (Phil. 1: 21–5) and adds later (3: 20) 'our commonwealth is in heaven, and from it we await a Saviour, the Lord Jesus Christ'. It is not until the Pastoral Epistles that the aged apostle seems to abandon the hope that he may himself live to see the Lord's appearing (2 Tim. 4: 6–8). God surely means the 'hope' of Christ's coming to burn brightly in the Church of all ages, until the day dawns.

The second event in the final drama is the resurrection of the body. The Thessalonian Christians had evidently been bereaved, and as many of them were expecting Jesus to return immediately they feared that those who had died would be at a disadvantage at His return. Paul hastens to reassure them. Far from losing, they would gain. 'The dead in Christ shall rise first' (4: 16). Then 'we who are alive . . . shall be caught up together with them in the clouds to meet the Lord in the air' (4: 17). Such survivors, still living at the time of the Lord's return, will 'be changed, in a moment, in the twinkling of an eye, at the last trumpet. For the trumpet will sound, and the dead will be raised incorruptible, and we shall be changed' (1 Cor. 15: 51–2). What will the resurrection body be like? It will not be a body miraculously reconstructed from the material particles of which it is at present composed. 'Flesh and blood cannot inherit the Kingdom of God' (1 Cor. 15: 50). It will be a new body, retaining its identity with the old, but as different from it as the flower is from the seed (1 Cor. 15: 35–41). It will be like the body of Christ's glory (Phil. 3: 21). The Lord's own resurrection will thus supply the pattern as well as the proof of ours (1 Cor. 15: 3–20). The body was 'sown in dishonour' (the seat of 'the flesh'); it will be 'raised in glory', no longer tainted by sin. It was 'sown in weakness', shackled by earthly limitations; it will be 'raised in power', invested with new and unknown capacities. It was sown 'a physical body' (adapted to biological life); it will be raised 'a spiritual body' (adapted to spiritual life). It was sown 'corruptible', subject to pain, disease, fatigue, decay and death; it will be raised 'incorruptible', enjoying imperishable youth, health and life (1 Cor. 15: 42–50). Meanwhile, in this body we 'groan', longing to be clothed with our new body (2 Cor. 5: 1–5). We are already redeemed in soul, but are eagerly awaiting the redemption of our bodies (Rom. 8: 18–25).

Then, thirdly, the end begins to come into view. The wicked, who 'know not God' and 'obey not the gospel of our Lord Jesus' will 'suffer the punishment of eternal destruction and exclusion from the presence of the Lord and from the glory of His might' (2 Thess. 1: 7–10). 'Let no man deceive you', Paul several times repeats, the wrath of God will fall on 'the sons of disobedience', and sinners shall not inherit God's Kingdom (cf. Eph. 5: 5–6; 1 Cor. 6: 9–10). And 'such things were some of you', he adds, monsters rather than men, 'but you were washed, you were sanctified, you were justified in the name of the Lord Jesus Christ and by the Spirit of our God' (1 Cor. 6: 11). It is 'Jesus who delivers us from the wrath to come' (1 Thess. 1: 10). Far from being excluded from His presence, 'we shall be ever with the Lord' (1 Thess. 4: 17). Now 'we walk by faith, not by sight' (2 Cor. 5: 7), but then we shall see Him. 'Now we see in a mirror dimly, but then face to face. Now I know in part; then I shall understand fully even as I have been fully understood' (1 Cor. 13: 12). Nor shall we enjoy fellowship with Him only. Heaven will be a place of glad reunion with one another as well. We shall be 'with them' as well as 'with the Lord' (1 Thess. 4: 17). Indeed, Christ 'died for us that whether we wake or sleep [that is, whether we die before He comes, or survive until His coming] we should live together, with Him' (1 Thess. 5: 10). Nor is that all. Nature itself will be redeemed. The very creation, which was temporarily subjected by God to futility and decay, is eagerly longing for 'the revealing of the sons of God', because it will then itself be 'set free from its bondage to decay and obtain the glorious liberty of the children of God' (Rom. 8: 18–22).

God's purpose is not only to have created 'all things' through Christ and for Christ (Col. 1: 16); not only to hold 'all things' together harmoniously in Christ (1: 17), but also in the fulness of time 'to unite all things in Him, things in heaven and things on earth' (Eph. 1: 10). 'Then comes the end, when He delivers the Kingdom to God the Father after destroying every rule and every authority and power . . . that God may be everything to every one' (1 Cor. 15: 24–8).

Such is God's purpose of grace for man, revealed through the Holy Spirit to the apostle Paul. Having himself had an experience of grace, he is given a theology of grace. Being able to say of himself: 'By the grace of God I am what I am' (1 Cor. 15: 10), he could marvel of others that they could so quickly desert Him who had called them in the grace of Christ (Gal. 1: 6). The same great purpose of grace which places us in Christ for acceptance, liberates us from indwelling sin, and unites us to one another in the Body of Christ, will preserve us to the end. 'He who hath begun a good work in you will bring it to completion at the day of Jesus Christ' (Phil. 1: 6).

Chapter IV

THE MESSAGE OF HEBREWS

This man, after He had offered one sacrifice for sins
for ever, sat down on the right hand of God.
                                        —Hebrews 10: 12

IF St. Luke teaches the universality of the gospel, and St. Paul its gratuity, the author of the Epistle to the Hebrews teaches its finality. His great theme is that Jesus Christ is God's last word to the world, that He has fulfilled all the Old Testament foreshadowings, and that there is nothing more to follow. Christianity is the perfect religion; it can never be superseded. Christ, through His eternal priesthood and unique sacrifice, has brought us an 'eternal salvation' (5: 9). We 'have come ... to Jesus, the mediator of a new covenant' (12: 22–4), which shall never pass away. Christ has ushered in 'the last days' (1: 2) and 'the end of the ages' (9: 26); we have only to await the consummation, when He shall appear again for final salvation and judgment (9: 28).

We can best understand the emphasis of this book by reconstructing the historical situation which called it forth. It was written to 'the Hebrews'. The title is not original, but it is almost certainly accurate. They were a definite, local Hebrew christian Church, for the author calls them 'brethren' (e.g., 3: 1 and 10: 19) and speaks of visiting them (13: 19, 23), and were probably 'in Jerusalem or in the neighbourhood of Jerusalem'.[1] These Jewish Christians were in grave danger of apostatizing, or 'drifting' (2: 1) away from Christ. It

[1] *The Epistle to the Hebrews*, by B.F. Westcott, p. xl. (Macmillan, 1889.)

was partly that they had been persecuted (e.g., 10: 32–9).
But it was more than that. They were intellectually at
sea. They could not understand how venerable Mosaic
institutions, ordained by God and hallowed by centuries, could be swept away. What was the relation
between the law and the gospel, between the new wine
and the old bottles? So our author writes to demonstrate
the superiority of Christ to all that had gone before.
His argument is theological, but his purpose is practical.
He longs to preserve them from apostasy. He will do
so by an exposition of the final supremacy of the priesthood, sacrifice and covenant of Jesus Christ, although
he will often break out into fervent appeals to them to
'hold fast' their 'profession' (3: 1; 4: 14; 10: 23).

Who, then, was the author? No one knows. Indeed,
the letter or treatise is really anonymous. The eastern
church from earliest years ascribed the letter to St. Paul.
So, from the time of Jerome and Augustine in the fifth
century did the west. John Owen, translator of Calvin,
said he 'entertained no more doubt on the subject than
if it had the apostle's own superscription'. Calvin himself however declared: 'I indeed can adduce no reason
to show that Paul was its author' and proceeded to
return to an earlier eastern suggestion that it had been
written by Luke or Clement. Barnabas was early thought
to be another possibility. Luther made the guess that
Apollos was the author, and certainly his Alexandrian
origin and knowledge of the Scriptures (Acts 18: 24)
would fit him to compose a work coloured by so many
Philonic (Alexandrian) ideas and Old Testament references. It is best to leave the matter in doubt, only adding
with Westcott[1] that 'we acknowledge the divine authority of the epistle'.

[1] ibid., p. lxxix.

All we know for certain about the author is what we can gather from his treatise. Even a casual reading of this makes it quite clear that he had a comprehensive grasp of the revealed facts associated with both the Old and the New Covenants. His work abounds in references both to the Old Testament Scriptures and to the gospel story. It is his intimate knowledge of these two parallel groups of facts which gives us the clue to his message. We must, therefore, consider the wealth of material at his disposal. Beginning with the Old Testament, he is able to quote from all five books of the Pentateuch, from Genesis (e.g., 4: 4=Gen. 2: 2), from Exodus (8: 5=Ex. 25: 40), from Leviticus (9: 7=Lev. 16), from Numbers (3: 5=Num. 12: 7) and from Deuteronomy (10: 30=Deut. 32: 35–6). He has a clear grasp of the historical setting of the books. He is familiar with the story of the creation (11: 3; 4: 4), the fall (6: 8), Cain and Abel (11: 4; 12: 24), Enoch who walked with God (11: 5–6), and the flood (11: 7). He refers to several events in the life of Abraham—his step of faith in leaving Ur (11: 8), his encounter with Melchizedek when returning from war with the Mesopotamian kings (7: 1–10), the promise of a son to aged Sarah (11: 11) and of a seed more numerous than the sand and the stars (11: 12; cf. 6: 13–15), the visit of the angels before the destruction of Sodom (13: 2), and his willingness to sacrifice Isaac (11: 17–19). He reminds his readers how Isaac blessed Jacob and Esau (11: 20), how Jacob bought the birthright (12: 16), how Esau pleaded with tears to have it back (12: 17), how Jacob crossed his hands when blessing Joseph's sons, Ephraim and Manasseh (11: 21), and how Joseph predicted the exodus from Egypt and gave directions about his burial (11: 22). He continues his reference to the history of God's

people by recounting the call of Moses, the exodus, the
Passover and the Sinaitic covenant (11: 23–9; 12: 18–21;
9: 18–21). He is well acquainted with the erection of
the Tabernacle and with all its furniture (9: 1–5), with
events during the forty years of wandering in the wilderness (3: 7–19), with the Levitical priesthood (7: 11)
and offerings (8: 3), and especially with the ritual of
both the Day of Atonement (9: 6–7; 13: 11–13) and the
red heifer (9: 13). He speaks of the settlement in the
promised land under Joshua (4: 8; cf. 13: 5), the fall of
Jericho (11: 30), and the rescue of the harlot, Rahab
(11: 31). He passes quickly over the period of the judges
but mentions Gideon, Barak, Samson, Jephthah and
Samuel by name (11: 32), and recalls, without elaboration, the stories of King David (11: 32), Elijah and the
widow of Zarephath or Elisha and the Shunammite
woman (11: 35), Daniel's escape from the den of lions
and his friends' from the burning fiery furnace (11:
33–4). He can quote with facility from the book of
Proverbs (12: 5–6); from the second book of Samuel
(1: 5); from the prophets Isaiah (2: 13), Jeremiah (8:
8–12), Ezekiel (13: 20), Hosea (13: 15), Habakkuk (10:
37–8), Haggai (12: 26) and Zechariah (13: 20); and from
no fewer than eleven different Psalms: 2 (1: 5), 8 (2: 6–8),
22 (2: 12), 40 (10: 5–7), 45 (1: 8–9), 95 (3: 7–11), 97 (1:
6), 102 (1: 10–12), 104 (1: 7), 110 (1: 13) and 118 (13: 6).

Such is our author's competent grasp of the Old
Testament. He is similarly well informed concerning
the career of Jesus. He refers to His incarnation (2: 14),
to His temptation (2: 18; 4: 15), to His ministry of
preaching (2: 3) and to His miracles (2: 4). Jesus is the
Shepherd (13: 20), as He styled Himself, and was faithful in obedience to God's will (3: 1–6; 10: 5–7). He
agonized in prayer 'with loud cries and tears to Him

who was able to save Him from death' (5: 7–8), and offered up Himself freely as a sacrifice (7: 27). He died (2: 9), and that by crucifixion (6: 6), outside the gate of the city (13:12), and was abused by His enemies (12: 3). His blood-shedding (9: 12, 14) ratified the new covenant of forgiveness (8: 8; 9: 15; 10: 18, 29; 12: 24; 13: 20). He was raised from the dead (13: 20, cf. 6: 2), 'passed through the heavens' (4: 14), 'sat down at the right hand of the Majesty on high' (1: 3; 10: 12), gave the Holy Spirit (2: 4; 6: 4) and will appear again for final salvation (9: 28) and judgment (10: 27).

Our author, whatever his identity, has therefore been well fitted by the Holy Spirit to teach the supersession of the Old Covenant by the New. He cannot be accused of ignorance or prejudice. He knows the facts about both, and that intimately. He is in a position to declare that the new wine has burst the old bottles.

(i) THE PRIESTHOOD OF CHRIST

He begins by demonstrating the superiority of the person of Christ to all other persons, angelic and human, particularly with regard to His priesthood. He writes of a fourfold superiority—to the prophets (1: 1–3) and the angels (1: 4–2: 18), to Moses (chs. 3–4) and to Aaron (chs. 5–7). The prophets and the angels were agents of *revelation*, for through the prophets God spoke to the fathers (1: 1) and through the angels He gave the law (2: 2). Moses and Aaron, on the other hand, were agents of *redemption*, Moses because he was God's 'apostle' (3: 1), sent (Ex. 3: 10) to Pharaoh to deliver the Israelites from bondage, and Aaron because he was the first high priest, appointed 'to act on behalf of men in relation to God, to offer gifts and sacrifices for sins' (5: 1). Jesus Christ is superior to all four.

When God spoke of old to the fathers, it was through the prophets 'in many parts [piecemeal] and in many ways' (1: 1), but now in these last days He has spoken to us finally and absolutely in His Son. His Son is not just a mouthpiece of God as the prophets were. He is 'the effulgence of His glory' (guaranteeing the community of His nature with the Father) and 'the image of His essence' (guaranteeing the distinctness of His person from the Father). Heir of all things, agent of creation, upholder of the universe, purifier of sins, He now sits at the right hand of the Majesty on high (1: 2–3). It is this exalted Son, unrivalled in the dignity of His person and work, in whom the final revelation has been given.

He is not only greater than the prophets; He is also greater than the angels. Indeed, He is 'as much superior to angels as the name He has obtained is more excellent than theirs' (1: 4). A chain of Old Testament passages is then added in which Christ's superiority as 'Son' to the angels is demonstrated (1: 5–14). Moreover, another Psalm testifies to the same truth, although in a more roundabout manner. Psalm 8 declares that God has made man 'for a little while lower than the angels' in order to crown him with glory and honour, and subject everything to him. This cannot refer to man now, argues the writer, because all things are not in subjection to him. Therefore it must refer to the Man Christ Jesus, for indeed we do see Him 'crowned with glory and honour' (2: 5–9). It also explains why in the process He needed to be made 'for a little while lower than the angels'. He is the Son of God *par excellence*. It was therefore fitting that the Father, wishing to bring other 'sons' to glory, should 'make the pioneer of their salvation perfect through suffering'. As our elder Brother, therefore, Jesus took our nature of flesh and blood in order to die and thereby to destroy the devil who has the power of death (2: 10–18). He was honoured not in spite of, but because of, His sufferings!

At the beginning of chapter 3 the author asks us to consider Jesus for ourselves, and describes Him as 'the apostle and high priest of our profession'. By this phrase he points to the superiority of Jesus to Moses, the great Old Testament 'apostle' and to Aaron, the great Old Testament 'high priest'. Now 'Moses was faithful in God's house' (3: 2). So was Jesus. But Moses represented only the house, whereas Jesus represented the builder (3: 3–4). Again, the faithfulness of Moses was that of a servant; the faithfulness of Jesus was that of a Son. Again, Moses' ministry was forward-looking; the benefits of Jesus' ministry may be enjoyed now (3: 5–6). The writer breaks into a long and fervent appeal. If dire penalties fell upon those who rebelled in the days of Moses, we must not harden our hearts against the Greater than Moses. 'Good news has come to us just as to them' (4: 2). If they did not enter into God's rest through unbelief, we must 'strive to enter that rest, that no one fall by the same sort of disobedience' (4: 11, cf. 3: 7–4: 13).

Christ is not only greater than Moses, as 'Apostle' of redemption or 'Captain of salvation' (3: 1; 2: 10). As High Priest He is also greater than Aaron (5: 1–10 and ch. 7).

Here we are approaching the heart of the argument. First, the writer is content to say that Jesus is like Aaron, since He was appointed by God to the office and not self-appointed (5: 1–6). Indeed, 'in the days of His flesh' Jesus subordinated Himself to the will of God and 'learned obedience through what He suffered', as is most clearly seen in the agony in the garden (5: 7–10).

Twice already in this passage, however, there has been introduced a phrase which will occupy an important place in the writer's later thought. It is a quotation from Psalm 110:4. It suggests that the priesthood of Jesus was superior to that of Aaron, because He was appointed a priest not after the order of Aaron but 'after the order of Melchizedek' (5: 6, 10). He then digresses again from 5: 11–6: 20, and one detects a note of righteous impatience in his words. He has much to say to his readers about the glories of the priesthood of Jesus after the order of Melchizedek, but it is hard to explain and his readers are backward and ignorant. They still need a diet of milk like children, instead of being able to digest solid food (5: 11–6: 3). He then warns them in the most solemn terms of the dangers of apostasy (6: 4–8), declares that he is sure they will themselves stand fast and inherit God's promises (6: 9–12), and encourages them to consider how immutable God's promises are (6: 13–20). Then he comes back to Melchizedek.

Melchizedek is a shadowy figure in the Old Testament. Apart from Psalm 110, from which our author has already quoted twice, he only appears in Genesis 14: 17–20. He was an ancient king of Jerusalem, and 'a priest of the most high God' (Gen. 14: 18). When Abraham had rescued Lot from a confederacy of Mesopotamian kings, Melchizedek came out to greet the victor, pronounced a formal blessing over him and accepted from him a tenth of the spoil (14: 19–20). There is much in this priest of long ago which prefigures the priesthood of Jesus. To begin with, his very name means 'righteousness', and he was king of Salem (i.e., Jerusalem) which means 'peace' (7: 2). Then again, he steps on to the scene in the Genesis story without any

introduction. We read nothing of his birth or death or
parentage or genealogy, and in this he symbolizes the
everlasting priesthood of the Son of God (7: 3). 'Thou
art a priest *for ever* after the order of Melchizedek.'
Having mentioned the features which are suggestive of
the priesthood of Jesus, our author continues by
demonstrating the superiority of his priesthood to that
of Aaron. It must be remembered that Aaron was
descended from Levi, and Levi from Abraham. As
Abraham and Melchizedek confront one another, therefore, the writer sees the two priesthoods contrasted,
Aaron's and Melchizedek's. Which was the greater? It
was Melchizedek's, and that for two reasons. Firstly,
because Melchizedek conferred a blessing on Abraham,
'and it is beyond dispute that the inferior is blessed by
the superior' (7: 7). Secondly, because Melchizedek received tithes from Abraham. Later, the Levitical priests
themselves received tithes from the Israelites, but here
they pay them through Abraham to Melchizedek (7:
4–10). So the priesthood of Melchizedek is greater than
the priesthood of Aaron. To this priesthood Jesus belongs, because in any case He was descended from Judah
and not from the priestly house of Levi (7: 13–14).
Therefore, the old priesthood has been superseded (7:
11–12), and Jesus enjoys an eternal priesthood like
Melchizedek's (7: 15–19), by a divine oath which can
never be rescinded (7: 20–2). The old Levitical priests
kept being replaced, because death prevented them from
continuing in office, but Jesus holds His priesthood
permanently because He lives for ever. Consequently,
He is able to save all who draw near to God through
Him, since He ever lives to make intercession for them
(7: 20–5).

Our author pauses at this stage in his argument. He

has described the essential qualities of the perfect high priest. He has indicated that Jesus Christ possessed these qualities. So he proceeds (8: 1), 'Now the point in what we are saying is this: we have such a high priest. . . .' Having established the final supremacy of His priesthood, he passes on to a consideration of His sacrifice (7: 26–10: 18). 'Every high priest is appointed to offer gifts and sacrifices; hence it is necessary for this priest also to have something to offer' (8: 3). It will be found that His work is as unique as His person.

THE SACRIFICE OF JESUS

Jesus Christ is the priest. What is the sacrifice? The author states that He must have something to offer, but delays a chapter before declaring what the sacrifice is. It is Himself. It is His own blood which is shed. He is the victim as well as the priest (9: 12, 14; 10 :10). In describing the character of Christ's offering of Himself, the writer refers to the Old Testament Levitical sacrifices. If Melchizedek's person typifies His priesthood, Aaron's offerings typify His sacrifice. He emphasizes particularly the ritual of the great annual Day of Atonement which is set out in Leviticus 16 (9: 1–5). He assumes that his readers are well acquainted with the design of the Tabernacle. It was divided into two compartments. The first and larger was the Holy Place. The further and smaller was the Holy of Holies, the inner sanctuary. Here stood the ark, surmounted by its golden lid the mercy seat, where the Shekinah glory, the visible symbol of God's presence, appeared. The two were separated by a thick curtain called the veil. By this arrangement the Holy One of Israel was teaching His people His presence among them and yet His inaccessibility to them. He was near and yet far. Sinners were not permitted to penetrate into His holy presence beyond the veil. Access to God was limited by four conditions which are listed in 9: 7. Only the High Priest might enter the inner sanctuary; but only once a year (on the Day of Atonement); and that only taking the blood of sacrifice; and then he would secure remission only of ceremonial defilement ('for the errors of the people', 9: 7). This signified that 'the way into the sanctuary is not yet opened' (9: 8). But Jesus Christ has opened the way into heaven, the perfect sanctuary (9: 12; 8: 2, 5), and the writer proceeds, point by point, to show how Christ's perfect sacrifice has fulfilled the imperfect foreshadowing of the Day of Atonement. We may take the four limitations in the opposite order. Christ's achievement is summarized in 9: 12: 'He entered once for all into the Holy Place not through the blood of bulls and calves but His own blood, thus securing an eternal redemption.'

(i) _The sphere of the sacrifice_ is not ceremonial but moral. He died not for the errors, but for the sins of the people. His blood cleanses not the flesh but the conscience (9: 9–10, 13–14). He has secured an 'eternal redemption'.

(ii) _The nature of the sacrifice._ It was His own blood, which could take away sins as the blood of bulls and goats could not (9: 13; 10: 4). What then is there so efficacious in the shedding of Christ's blood? Many commentators have found the answer in the words which describe Christ as offering Himself 'through the (or an) eternal spirit' to God (9: 14). A. B. Bruce calls it 'the most important expression of the whole epistle'[1] and writes elsewhere: 'The magic phrase . . . lifts us

---

[1] *The Epistle to the Hebrews: The First Apology for Christianity*, by A. B. Bruce, p. 327 ad loc. (T. & T. Clark, 1899.)

above distinctions of time and place, and makes it possible for us to regard Christ's offering of Himself, in all its stages, as a transaction within the heavenly sanctuary.'[1] That Christ should have offered Himself, and made the offering 'through an eternal spirit', makes the sacrifice conscious in its purpose, moral in its character, and eternal in its effect. But it is still not clear how the sacrifice avails for the remission of sin. Indeed, the writer never explains exactly wherein lies the efficacy of His death. But there are significant pointers which we must consider. The cross is seen as part of God's eternal purpose to 'bring many sons to glory' (2: 10). It is therefore true to say not only that He 'offered Himself' (9: 14) but that He 'was offered' (9: 28). This last verse goes on to define the purpose of the offering. It was 'to bear the sins of many'. This is the only occasion in the epistle where Christ's sacrifice is described in terms of sin bearing, but it cannot for that reason be set aside. He succeeded in 'putting away sin by the sacrifice of Himself' (9: 26) because He Himself bore the sins of many. The phrase has many Old Testament links. To 'bear sin' in the book of Leviticus is to suffer the consequences and undergo the penalty of sin. 'If a soul sin and commit any of these things which are forbidden to be done by the commandments of the Lord . . . he is guilty and shall bear his iniquity' (Lev. 5: 17). Of the sin offering it is written, however: 'God hath given it to you to bear the iniquity of the congregation to make atonement for them before the Lord' (10: 17). The same is said of the living 'scapegoat' on the Day of Atonement: 'and the goat shall bear upon him all their iniquities' (16: 22). It is this element of sinbearing in sacrifice which recurs in the great portrayal

[1] ibid., pp. 295-6.

of the Suffering Servant of the Lord who is described in Isaiah as being 'wounded for our transgressions' (53: 5) and as bearing the iniquities of his people (53: 11–12, cf. 6). This prophecy our Lord took to Himself, interpreting His death in terms of it. To it also the writer to the Hebrews refers when he says: 'He was once offered to bear the sins of many' (Heb. 9: 28).

It is in this connexion that we are to understand the symbolism of bloodshedding which is so common in the Epistle. New Testament commentators have often maintained that the shedding of Christ's blood signifies the life of Christ liberated by death and made available for the use of others. Thus 'the Scriptural idea of blood is essentially an idea of life and not of death . . . The blood poured out is the energy of present human life made available for others.[1] The Rev. A. M. Stibbs has recently shown, however, in his Tyndale Monograph, *The Meaning of the Word 'Blood' in Scripture* (1947), that this is a mistaken conviction. He quotes J. Armitage Robinson, Kittel's *Theological Dictionary* and others, and examines carefully the Biblical evidence to show that 'blood' means not 'life' but 'death', and that, violent death. More accurately, the blood is the life (Gen. 9: 4; Lev. 17: 11), but it is the life laid down in death, not the life lived before death or released after death. 'So the term "the blood of Christ" is a metaphorical or symbolical way of referring to His early death in a human body upon a cross of shame, and to its innumerable and eternal consequences. And it is these benefits of His passion that are meant to be conveyed to and enjoyed by all who are said . . . to be sprinkled by His blood.'[2]

---

[1] Westcott, op. cit., pp. 295–6.
[2] *The Meaning of the Word 'Blood' in Scripture*, by A. M. Stibbs, p. 21. (Tyndale Press, 1947.)

(iii) *The uniqueness of the sacrifice.* The High Priest took the blood of sacrifice into the sanctuary every year on the Day of Atonement. The priests offered repeatedly, day after day, year after year, the same sacrifices. Christ died once. This word 'once', signifying not 'once upon a time' but 'once for all' is a favourite word of our author's. It recurs constantly in the section stretching from 9: 11 to 10: 14. 'He has appeared once for all to put away sin by the sacrifice of Himself' (9: 26). He was 'once offered to bear the sins of many' (9: 28). 'We have been sanctified through the offering of the body of Jesus Christ once for all' (10: 10). 'Christ . . . offered for all time a single sacrifice for sins . . . for by a single offering He has perfected for all time those who are sanctified' (10: 12, 14).

(iv) *The achievement of the sacrifice.* Under the Levitical law the sacred privilege of access to the Divine Presence within the sanctuary was restricted to the High Priest, representing the people. None other might approach. But Jesus, our great High Priest, entered into the heavenly sanctuary not just as our representative but as our forerunner (6: 20). Not only has He been 'crowned with glory' (2: 9), but desires to 'bring many sons to glory' (2: 10). The veil has been done away. Any sinner sprinkled by the blood of Jesus (cf. 10: 19–22; 12: 24) may 'draw near to God' (7: 19, 25) and 'draw near to the throne of grace' (4: 16).

The writer is now in a position to introduce his principal theme. This unique Person through His unique work has established a unique covenant. As the author has demonstrated the superiority of Jesus Christ to prophets and angels, Moses and Aaron, and as he has shown the superiority of His sacrifice to all the Levitical offerings, he now proceeds to describe the superiority of the New Covenant which Christ has established.

3 THE NEW COVENANT

The subject, which he has already mentioned in chapters 7 and 8, is unfolded with clear logic in 9, 15 *et seqq*. The writer has finished his exposition of the uniqueness of Christ's divine person and saving work. He now continues: 'Therefore He is the mediator of a new covenant.' Further, this 'new' covenant is a 'better' covenant (7: 22), because its terms are better than the terms of the old. 'It is enacted on better promises' (8: 6). If the terms of the 'first covenant had been faultless, there would have been no occasion for a second' (8: 7, 13). The terms of this fresh and better agreement between God and man had been foretold through the prophet Jeremiah (Jer. 31: 31–4) and are quoted by our author twice (8: 8–12; 10: 16–17). They set forth God's gracious threefold promise to write His laws on the hearts and minds of His people, to reveal Himself to each individually and to forgive their sins. It is our writer's purpose to show that this promise of inward holiness, personal knowledge and full forgiveness has been fulfilled through our Saviour's death. He uses three approaches First, he resorts to a human illustration. The Greek and Hebrew words for a 'covenant' can also mean a 'will' or 'testament'. Thus, as a will takes effect only when the testator dies, so the New Testament came into force only when Jesus died (9: 15–17). Secondly, he uses a Biblical analogy. He declares that as the first, Mosaic covenant was ratified with blood, so the New Covenant was inaugurated by the blood of Jesus, which is 'the blood of the covenant' (9: 18–21; 10: 29; 13: 20;

cf. Mt. 26: 28). He concludes, thirdly, with a theological argument. The New Covenant promises forgiveness, but 'without shedding of blood there is no forgiveness' (9: 22). Therefore, it was Christ's atoning death which established the New Covenant. Moreover, now forgiveness is secured and the New Covenant is in force 'There is no longer any offering for sin' (10: 14–18).

It is to this finality of the New Covenant that the writer has been gradually leading us. God has spoken and acted finally in the person and work and covenant of Jesus Christ. There can be no question of other 'priests' in a sacrificial sense, since through our great High Priest we enjoy direct access to God and need no other mediator. There can be no question of other 'sacrifices for sin'. Our salvation has been achieved by His unique sacrifice. Our sacrifices are 'sacrifices of praise' (13: 15), not 'sacrifices for sin' (10: 18). They express our gratitude. They cannot, and do not need to, achieve our forgiveness. Again, there can be no question of another covenant. The 'new' covenant is the last covenant. The 'better' covenant is the best covenant. It will never be superseded. 'The law made nothing perfect' (7: 19), but Christ has 'perfected for all time those who are sanctified' (10: 14). The eternity of this final, perfect salvation seems to fill the writer's mind. Christ is a priest 'for ever' (5: 6; 6: 20; 7: 21) who has made 'one sacrifice for sins for ever' (10: 12) and thus established an 'eternal covenant' (13: 20) which brings to God's people an 'eternal salvation' (5: 9), 'an eternal redemption' (9: 12) and an 'eternal inheritance' (9: 15).

Only when we, with the first readers of the epistle, have grasped this majestic theme of the writer, are we in a position to understand its practical application.

Those Hebrew Christians were in danger of backsliding.
Exposed to vicious persecution and specious argument,
they were wavering in their Christian faith and con-
templating apostasy to Judaism. The author is illumined
by the Holy Spirit to teach the finality of the Christian
covenant. If it is final, he argues, it must be held fast.
It is inconceivable that his readers should drift back into
the Old Covenant.

(4)   EXHORTATION

Having concluded his exposition of the unique person, work and covenant of Christ, he continues:
'Therefore, brethren' (10: 19–25), 'since we have confidence to enter the sanctuary by the blood of Jesus . . .
and since we have a great priest over the house of God',
and he proceeds to elaborate his threefold appeal to
faith ('let us draw near . . . in full assurance of faith'),
hope ('let us hold fast the confession of our hope without wavering') and love ('let us consider how to stir
up one another to love and good works'). He digresses
during the rest of chapter 10 (vv. 26–39) to give his
readers both warning and encouragement, and then
returns to his appeal. It is difficult to analyse the last
three chapters, but they appear to develop this threefold
theme, as chapter 11 lays emphasis on faith, chapter 12
on hope and chapter 13 on love.

Faith is 'the assurance of things hoped for, the conviction of things not seen' (11: 1). We are not to 'shrink
back' but to 'live by faith' (10: 38), drawing near to God
like the heroes of the Old Testament. By faith they both
received God's promises and obeyed His commands.
'Surrounded by so great a cloud of witnesses' we also
must 'lay aside every weight and sin which clings so

closely' and 'run with perseverance the race which is set before us, looking to Jesus the pioneer and perfecter of our faith' (12: 1–2).

Those old-time heroes were men of hope as well as faith. Some promises of God they inherited in their lifetime by faith, but in another sense 'they did not receive what was promised' (11: 39). The earthly blessings they received typified spiritual blessings they did not receive. These blessings they awaited in hope, that is, in joyful and confident expectation. By hope, therefore, they endured. Christ also 'endured the cross because of the joy which was set before Him' (12: 2). We should 'consider Him who endured' lest we 'grow weary or faint-hearted', and remember that it is for discipline that we have to endure, since God disciplines His beloved children (12: 3–11). Therefore we are to lift our drooping hands and strengthen our weak knees (12: 12) and beware lest we do not endure to the end, for we have come not to the Old Covenant inaugurated with 'fire and darkness, gloom and a tempest' but to 'Jesus, the mediator of a new covenant' (12: 18–24).

The last chapter touches briefly on various aspects of brotherly love (13: 1). We are to be hospitable to strangers (13: 2), to remember the prisoners (13: 3), to honour marriage (13: 4), to prefer contentment to covetousness (13: 5), and to respect our Christian leaders (13: 7–9, 17, 24). We are to go forth to Jesus 'outside the camp', where He suffered, and with the rest of God's worshipping people bear reproach for His sake (13: 10–15). We are to do good and share our possessions with those in need (13: 16), and pray for one another (13: 18–19). The writer ends his Epistle with an appeal to them as 'brethren' to bear his 'word of exhortation', to greet all their leaders and all the saints, and he prays that God's grace may be with them all (13: 22–5).

All these Christian privileges and obligations, of access to God by faith, of endurance through hope and of brotherly love within the Church, issue from the great fact our writer has been at pains to emphasize. They depend on the final covenant of eternal salvation. 'Having therefore, brethren, boldness to enter into the holiest by the blood of Jesus . . . let us draw near . . . in faith, let us hold fast . . . our hope . . . let us consider one another to provoke unto love . . .' (10: 19–25).

Chapter V

THE MESSAGE OF JAMES

I will show thee my faith by my works.—James 2: 18

A T least three men with the name 'James' appear in the pages of the New Testament. There was James, the son of Zebedee and brother of John, one of the Twelve. He was beheaded at the command of Herod Agrippa I (Acts 12: 1–2), so that he cannot have been the author of the Epistle of James. Then there was another member of the apostolic band called James. He was the son of Alphaeus (e.g., Mk. 3: 18), and is probably also James 'the Less' or 'the Little', who is mentioned, for instance, in Mark 15: 40. Our knowledge of him is very scanty, and it is unlikely that so obscure a person would have written a general epistle and introduced himself simply as 'James, a servant of God and of the Lord Jesus Christ' (1: 1) without further qualification or description. We are left with James, one of the Lord's brethren (Mk. 6: 3). It is not clear whether these men were His brothers or half-brothers or cousins. James became the most eminent member of the family. It is possible that he was the eldest, since he heads the list, 'James, Joseph, Simon and Judas' (Mt. 13: 55–6; Mk. 6: 3). He will have been brought up in that holiest and happiest of homes, and will have watched the matchless life of the Son of God. Yet, when the public ministry of Jesus began, James and the other 'brethren of the Lord' did not believe in Him (John 7:

5; cf. Lk. 4: 24; Mk. 3: 21, 31–35). It may have been that He seemed to them to disregard some of the commandments of the sacred law which they had been taught to love and revere. They evidently accompanied Him at different times during His ministry both in Galilee (Jn. 2: 12) and in Jerusalem (Jn. 7: 1–10), but they had not committed themselves to Him. It is remarkable, therefore, that during the ten days which elapsed between the Ascension and Pentecost, the Lord's brethren are specially mentioned by Luke as finding their place in the believing, praying company of expectant Christians (Acts 1: 14). Perhaps, at least in the case of James, the clue is given by St. Paul, who includes in his catalogue of those who saw the risen Lord the statement 'and He appeared unto James' (1 Cor. 15: 7). No account of this interview has survived, but it serves to explain how James became a believer.

He appears rapidly to have won the confidence of the others, and within a very short time he is acknowledged as the leader of the Jerusalem church (Acts 12: 17). He was never given the title 'bishop', but Eusebius, the fourth-century ecclesiastical historian, sees in him the first example of episcopacy and writes that it was to him that 'the apostles had entrusted the throne of the episcopate at Jerusalem'. St. Paul acknowledges him as an 'apostle' and states that he saw him on his first visit to Jerusalem within three years of his conversion, when he stayed a fortnight with Peter (Gal. 1: 18–19). About twelve years later (i.e., fourteen years after his conversion, Gal. 2: 1), he visited Jerusalem again, probably on the occasion when he and Barnabas brought famine-relief from the church of Antioch (cf. Acts 11: 27–30; 12: 25), and this time he had a special meeting with the leaders of the church, at the conclusion of which James,

Peter and John gave him and Barnabas the right hand of fellowship and confirmed their call to preach the gospel to the Gentiles. This is in fact what Paul and Barnabas did when, shortly after their return to Antioch, they set sail with Mark on the first missionary journey. During this journey many Gentiles believed. On their return to Antioch, a delegation of Jewish Christians 'came down from Judea' and 'taught the brethren, and said, Except ye be circumcised . . . ye cannot be saved' (Acts 15: 1). These men had come, or at least claimed to have come, 'from James' (Gal. 2: 12). The controversy became so sharp that Paul and Barnabas and Peter and some of the Jerusalem delegates determined to go 'unto the apostles and elders about this question' (Acts 15: 2). James took the chair at this important Council of Jerusalem reported by Luke in Acts 15, and through his wise deductions from Scripture and experience led the conference to the decision that circumcision was not necessary for the Gentile converts (Acts 15: 19). The apostolic decrees added, however, that such Gentile converts must abstain from idolatry and immorality and even from certain foods in accordance with regulations laid down in the law of Moses (Acts 15: 20–1, 28–9).

This same zeal for the Mosaic law is seen in the only other passage in the Acts which features James. Years had passed. Paul had completed two further missionary journies since the first. Hundreds of Gentiles had been converted and welcomed into the Church. They had been baptized but not circumcised. Paul had now returned to Jerusalem. The day following his arrival he and his fellow-missionaries called on James and told him of God's work among the Gentiles. James rejoiced, and glorified God. But he added a caution. He reminded

Paul that there were also thousands of Jewish believers who were 'zealous of the law'. They had heard the rumour that Paul was urging his Jewish converts to forsake Moses. So James made the suggestion that Paul should go with four others who had made a vow to God, and that together in the Temple they should perform the rites of purification required by the law of Moses. This would clearly demonstrate Paul's continued regard for, and obedience to, the sacred law of God. Paul readily consented (Acts 21: 17–26).

James is thus revealed in the Acts as a Jewish Christian believer, who was concerned that the acceptance of the new faith should not involve the complete abandonment of the old. The gospel of Jesus had fulfilled but not abrogated the law of Moses. It is not surprising therefore that James earned the nickname 'the Just'. Eusebius wrote: 'The philosophy and godliness, which his life displayed to so eminent a degree, was the occasion of a universal belief in him as the most just of men.' He goes on to quote Hegesippus who lived towards the end of the second century and who said that James was a Nazarite. 'He was in the habit of entering alone into the Temple, and was frequently found upon his knees begging forgiveness for the people, so that his knees became hard like those of a camel, in consequence of his constantly bending them in his worship of God, and asking forgiveness for the people. Because of his exceeding great justice he was called "the Just"....' According to the Jewish historian Josephus, and to Hegesippus, again quoted by Eusebius, James was later martyred in Jerusalem. He is said to have been cast down from the pinnacle of the Temple and then beaten to death with a club.

Such is the character of the man who contributed

what is probably the earliest of the New Testament documents. ~~Most commentators give the epistle a date not later than A.D. 50, and some believe it to have been written as early as A.D. 45.~~ It was written to Jewish Christians of the dispersion whose assembly was still called a 'synagogue' (James 2: 2) and who were apparently undergoing a hard time of testing.

The distinctive characteristic of the epistle, as we should expect from such a man as James, is his emphasis on the necessity of moral behaviour in the Christian life. The Holy Spirit fashioned his temperament and overruled his experience in order to convey this message through him. The atmosphere of the letter is reminiscent of the Old Testament prophets, and it 'reads like a collection of short homilies'.[1] The author uses more than fifty imperatives in his five short chapters, and is fond of moral aphorisms like 'a double-minded man is unstable in all his ways' (1: 8) and 'the friendship of the world is enmity with God' (4: 4). His use of vivid metaphor recalls the parabolic teaching of Jesus, and there is strong internal evidence that James heard both the Sermon on the Mount and other discourses of Jesus. As Robert Scott writes in *The Speaker's Commentary*, 'If John has lain on the Saviour's bosom, James has sat at His feet.' This subject is so interesting and important that it may be helpful to elaborate the comparison between the teaching of James and the teaching of Jesus.

The Christian who is called upon to suffer trial is 'blessed' (1: 2; Mt. 5: 10–12). God's purpose is that we may become perfect (1: 4; Mt. 5: 48). He gives generously to all who ask (1: 5; 4: 2; Mt. 7: 7–8), but the Father only gives good gifts (1: 17; Mt. 7: 9–11) and

[1] *Letters to Young Churches* by J. B. Phillips, p. 185. (Bles, 1947.)

then only to those who have faith (1: 6; Mk. 11: 22–4). The disciple must not only hear the word but do it (1: 22–5; Mt. 7: 21–7). He must beware of riches, because it is the poor who are heirs of the Kingdom (2: 5; Mt. 5: 3; Lk. 6: 20). He must love his neighbour as himself (2: 8; Mk. 12: 31); keep even the least of the commandments, not offending in one single point (2: 10; Mt. 5: 19); and show mercy if he would receive mercy (2: 13; Mt. 5: 7 and 18: 33–5). He must remember that it is the tree which determines the fruit (3: 12; Mt. 7: 15–20) and the peacemakers who are blessed (3: 18; Mt. 5: 9). No man can serve two masters. Each must choose between God and the world, between God and mammon (4: 4; Mt. 6: 24). He who humbles himself will be exalted (4: 6, 10; Lk. 18: 14; cf. Jas. 1: 9–10 and Lk. 1: 52). Christians must not speak evil of one another or judge one another (4: 11–12; Mt. 7: 1). They must not indulge in ambitious, worldly planning to get gain (4: 13–17; Lk. 12: 16–21), for wealth does not last. Riches rot, garments become motheaten, and gold tarnishes like rust (5: 1–3; Mt. 6: 19–21). Woe therefore to the rich (5: 1; Lk. 6: 24 and 16: 19–31). Let the believer wait patiently and be ready for the Lord's coming, for He is near, even at the gates (5: 7–9; Lk. 12: 35–40; Mk. 13: 29). Finally, the Christian brother must not swear at all, by heaven or by earth or with any other oath. His word must be reliable. His yes must be yes and his no, no (5: 12; Mt. 5: 33–7).

James 'the Just', faithfully echoing the ethical teaching of Jesus, gives detailed and practical advice about the life of believers. The man who ably took the chair at the Jerusalem conference (Acts 15) and urged Paul to conciliate the Jews who were 'all zealous for the law' (Acts 21: 17–26), now reminds his Jewish Christian readers that the moral law is still binding upon God's people. It must be kept in every point (2: 10–13). Indeed, the new law of Jesus is a 'perfect law' and a 'law of liberty' (1: 25; 2: 12). Above all, Christians must fulfil 'the royal law' (2: 8), the law governing the citizens of God's Kingdom (2: 5), namely: 'Thou shalt love thy neighbour as thyself.' First promulgated through Moses (Lev. 19: 18), then sanctioned by Jesus (Mk. 12: 31), this law is still in force. God is not impressed by our religious knowledge or outward profession. He desires obedience and inward sincerity. It is not enough to hear the word. We must do it. Hearing the word and failing to do it is as senseless as looking in the mirror, seeing (for instance) that one is untidy, and then forgetting to brush one's hair and clean one's face (1: 22–5). To know what is right and not to do it is sin (4: 17). It is no use claiming to have faith if one has no good works. Such faith, if it is by itself and has no good works, is dead. It is not real faith at all.

Paul and James have been thought to contradict one another. Abraham was justified not by works but by faith, Paul wrote in Romans 4: 2–3. 'Was not Abraham our father justified by works . . . ?' asks James in 2: 21. It is well known that Martin Luther, living in an age of controversy when the great doctrine of justification by faith had just been rediscovered, repudiated the epistle of James, adding contemptuously that it was made of 'straw'. The contradiction between the two apostles is, however, purely imaginary. The New Testament represents them as recognizing each other's place in God's purpose for the Church. James had welcomed Paul's mission to the Gentiles (Gal. 2: 9), and Paul had respected James's concern for Jewish feeling (Acts 21: 17–26). The two men were given a different ministry but not a different message. They proclaimed the same gospel, but with a different emphasis.

The reason for this different emphasis is not far to seek. They had a different set of false teachers in mind. Paul's opponents were the Jewish legalists. James's were the Jewish intellectualists. According to the legalists the way of salvation was 'works'—moral and ceremonial acts performed in obedience to the law. According to the intellectualists the way of salvation was 'faith', by which they meant mere orthodoxy of belief. To the legalists Paul argues that we are justified not by our own good works but through faith in Christ. To the intellectualists James argues that we are justified not by a barren orthodoxy (which even the demons possess— 'and shudder'! 2: 19), but by works. Paul, however, is swift to add that the faith which saves issues inevitably in good works (Eph. 2: 8–10; Gal. 5: 6), while James affirms that the works which save spring naturally from a true faith (2: 15). We are, in fact, saved neither by dead faith (Jas. 2: 17) nor by dead works (Heb. 6: 1; 9: 14) but by a living faith which results in 'love and good works' (Heb. 10: 24). We cannot be saved by works. Yet we cannot be saved without works. The place of works is not to earn salvation but to evidence it, not to procure salvation, but to prove it. The reality of one's faith is revealed in the quality of one's life. 'Good works . . . do spring out necessarily of a true and lively faith; insomuch that by them a lively faith may be as evidently known as a tree discerned by the fruit' (Articles of the Church of England, No. 12—Of Good Works). Abraham's faith was of this calibre. He trusted God's promises, and therefore he obeyed God's command (Jas. 2: 21–4). He practised 'the obedience of faith',—a phrase which Paul employs (Rom. 16: 26). The Holy

H

Spirit uses Paul to stress the faith which results in works, and James to stress the works which result from faith.

The most illuminating summary of James's theme is to be found in 1: 26–7. In these verses he again draws the contrast between true and false religion, but in different terms. Now it is not the distinction between 'hearing' and 'doing' (1: 22–5), nor between 'saying' and 'hearing' (2: 14–20), but between 'thinking' and 'being'. A man may imagine himself to be religious, but unless his religion is accompanied by morality he is deceiving himself and his religion is vain. James then outlines the three characteristics of real religion, which he calls 'pure and undefiled'. They are to 'bridle the tongue', to 'visit orphans and widows' and to 'keep oneself unstained from the world'. This is a penetrating analysis of the moral duty of man. It includes his three-fold duty to himself, to his neighbour and to his God. Tongue-control is an index to self-control. The visitation of orphans and widows is an example of brotherly love. To keep oneself unstained from the world is the negative counterpart to giving God the worship due to His name. The rest of James's epistle contains variations on this threefold theme.

SELF-CONTROL

Having urged his readers in his first chapter (1: 19–21) to be 'quick to hear' but 'slow to speak', James enlarges on the dangerous influence of the tongue in the celebrated passage in chapter 3 (1–12). The tongue is the smallest member, but it is the hardest to tame. The man, therefore, who has learned to bridle his tongue is 'able to bridle the whole body also' (3: 2). But the tongue is hard to tame. We can tame every kind of beast and bird, reptile and fish, but 'no human being can tame the tongue' (3: 7). He seems to imply that only God can. We are not surprised at his conclusion when we read his account of the tongue's baneful influence. He adds image to image in vivid, descriptive pen pictures. The tongue 'stains' the body, and 'ignites the wheel of nature' (3: 6), that is, probably, the whole course of human life. It is a 'restless evil', 'full of deadly poison' (3: 8). Its power is out of all proportion to its size. Just as a small bit in a horse's mouth controls the horse; and as a little rudder enables the pilot to steer a great, storm-tossed ship; and as a tiny spark can set a vast forest ablaze; so 'the tongue is a little member and boasts great things' (3: 3–5). How can we, out of the same mouth, bless God and curse men? Do salt water and fresh water flow from the same spring? Can figs and olives grow on the same tree, or grapes and figs? 'My brethren, these things ought not so to be' (3: 9–12). We must guard the tongue, and not aspire too readily to be teachers, lest we cannot control our tongue (3: 1).

Despite James's elaborate reference to the tongue, he was clearly using it as an example only. The origin of temptation is not the tongue. The trouble is more deep-seated still. Temptation comes not from God (who can neither tempt nor be tempted, 1: 13), but from man's inward desire. He does not tell us exactly whence the desire comes. St. Paul would have called it 'the flesh'. This 'lust' produces sin, and sin death (1: 14–15). We are to resist such temptations and to put away from our lives all filthiness and wickedness (1: 21).

Although temptations are to be resisted, trials are to be welcomed (1: 2). The Greek word for 'temptation' and 'trial' is the same, but the meaning is different. A temptation is an enticement to sin which arises from within. A trial is a testing of faith which comes from some external circumstance such as persecution. The value of such trials is that they develop Christian character and 'produce steadfastness' (1: 3–4).

② THE ROYAL LAW

The second element in 'pure and undefiled' religion is love. Paul and James are agreed that faith engenders love. James affirms that a man who says he has faith and yet leaves a brother or sister without adequate food and clothing, has no real faith at all (2: 14–17). Paul states the corresponding positive truth that faith works through love (Gal. 5: 6).

This reveals the first characteristic of true Christian love, namely, that it leads to action. Pious benevolence is no substitute for practical kindness. It is no good sympathizing with orphans and widows; we must visit them (1: 27). It is useless to say to a beggar: 'Be warmed and filled'; we must give him food and clothing (2: 15–16). As John wrote later: 'Little children, let us not love in word or speech, but in deed and in truth' (1 Jn. 3: 18). Christian love is not sentiment but service, not affection but action. Love's activity is varied. It leads not only to kind deeds towards a brother but to kind words also. We may not speak evil against one another or judge one another (4: 11–12). Our words must be dependable (5: 12). Love will also show itself in meekness. It will neither boast, nor envy, nor quarrel. It is peaceable. This is the wisdom which comes from above (3: 13–18). Further, love seeks the sinner's restoration, and desires not to expose but rather to cover his brother's sins (5: 19–20).

It will have been noticed how often James refers to

the 'brother' and the 'neighbour' when writing of the
duties of love. These words introduce the second
characteristic of true Christian love, namely, its im-
partiality. Love recognizes no distinctions and abhors
'respect of persons'. It appears that the Jewish Christian
assemblies to which James is addressing his letter were
composed largely of poorer people. He imagines what
would happen if some well-to-do personage were to
come to Sunday worship dressed in fine clothing. He
deprecates the servile flattery which would be given him,
while the shabbily dressed worshippers would have to
give place and sit on the floor. Such class distinctions
are wholly inconsistent with the royal law. 'Don't ever
attempt, my brothers, to combine snobbery with faith
in our Lord Jesus Christ!' (Jas. 2: 1–9).[1]

DUTY TO GOD

Mention of the rich leads to the third element in 'pure
and undefiled' religion. It is to 'keep oneself unstained
from the world'. James places God and 'the world' in
opposition to one another, as Jesus did God and
'mammon'. John, too, writes that the love of the Father
and the love of the world are incompatible (1 Jn. 2:
15–17). By 'the world' he means materialistic, pagan
society, with its empty pleasures and godless standards.
The Christian must choose. Our prayers are often un-
answered because our motives are wrong and our
ambitions selfish (4: 1–3). We are guilty of the same
spiritual adultery of which the prophets accused ancient
Israel. Married to God, we yet flirt with the world. Do
we not know that 'friendship with the world is enmity
with God'? God is 'jealous' towards us, yearning for

[1] J. B. Phillips, op. cit., p. 187.

our undivided love. The danger of riches is that they absorb too much of our attention. Further, many of the rich become both oppressors of God's people (2: 6) and blasphemers of God's name (2: 7). They will finally pass away as the grass withers under a scorching sun (1: 9–11), and their riches will perish with them (5: 1–6). Let the Christian rather be 'rich in faith' and rejoice that he is 'an heir of the Kingdom' (2: 5). Let him find his wealth in God. Let him not make rash plans for selfish gain, without reference to God (4: 13–17). Let him humble himself before the Lord (4: 10), submit himself to God (4: 7), be filled with prayers and praises (5: 13–18) and be patient 'until the coming of the Lord' (5: 7–11).

The Christian life, according to James 'the Just', is thus essentially a life of practical holiness. It begins indeed with 'faith in our Lord Jesus Christ' (2: 1), but the Christian adds: 'I will show you my faith by my works' (2: 18).

Chapter VI

THE MESSAGE OF JOHN

*These are written that you may believe that Jesus is
the Christ, the Son of God, and that believing you may
have life in His name.*—John 20: 31

*I write this to you who believe in the name of the Son
of God, that you may know that you have eternal life.*
1 John 5: 13

THERE are five separate documents in our New Testament which are attributed to the authorship of John,
namely, the gospel bearing his name, the three epistles,
and the Revelation. Of these, the Revelation is so
different in subject-matter that it must receive separate
treatment, whether or not it was written by the same
John. The gospel and the epistles, however, as is now
almost universally agreed, come from the pen of the
same author. Not only is the Greek style greatly similar,
but there are many striking theological phrases which
are common to both, like 'Spirit of truth', 'light' and
'darkness', 'of the world', 'children of God', 'abiding in'
Christ, 'keeping His commandments', 'love', 'witness',
'life' and 'death'.

But who was the author? It is a complicated and
controversial question. Many books have been written
on the subject. The traditional view that the gospel and
epistles were written in his old age at Ephesus by John
the son of Zebedee is still upheld by some scholars and
cannot be lightly dismissed. The most convincing ex-

position of the internal evidence for this view remains that of Bishop Westcott, whose commentary on St. John appeared in 1908 but was written a number of years previously. He argues in gradually narrowing concentric circles, as follows:

1. The author was a Jew. His Greek style has Aramaic peculiarities. 'The words are Greek words but the spirit by which they live is Hebrew.' His vocabulary, syntax and imagery reveal traces of Hebrew influence. He quotes from the Old Testament to show the fulfilment of prophecy (e.g., 19: 24, 28, 36–7), but is not tied to the Septuagint (the Greek version of the Old Testament). He is conversant with Jewish customs (e.g., 2: 6; 3: 25; 10: 22; 18: 28; 19: 31). 'His special knowledge, his literary style, his religious faith all point to the same conclusion.'

2. The author was 'a Palestinian Jew of the first century'. He is familiar with the religious parties and controversies of the day and distinguishes between 'the Pharisees' and 'the High Priests' (Sadducees). He also knows intimately the geography of Palestine and especially of Jerusalem and the Temple before its destruction. 'He moves about in a country which he knows' (e.g., 1: 28; 2: 1, 11; 3: 23; 4: 5–6; 5: 2–3; 8: 20; 9: 7; 10: 22–3; 11: 18, 54; 18: 1, 28; 19: 13, 17, 20).

3. The author was an eyewitness. He is acquainted not only with the places which he mentions, but with the events which took place there. He describes 'minute details of persons, and time, and place and manner, which cannot but have come from a direct experience'.

4. The author was an apostle. 'This follows almost necessarily from the character of the scenes which he describes', and from his knowledge of the feelings of the disciples and from the fact of his nearness to the Lord. He must, for instance, have been present at least

some of the time when Jesus turned the water into wine
(2: 1–11), spoke to the Samaritan woman (4: 1–43),
healed the man born blind (ch. 9), raised Lazarus from
the dead (ch. 11), washed the disciples' feet (13: 1–12),
and was arrested, tried and crucified (chs. 18–19). These
graphic descriptions are those of an eyewitness who
must have been an apostle.

5. The author was the apostle John. The author is
stated to be 'the disciple whom Jesus loved' (21: 20, 24),
although that verse appears to be an appended note by
another and later writer ('we know that his testimony
is true'). But who is the beloved disciple who is mentioned in 13: 23; 19: 26; 20: 2; 21: 7, 20, and who appears
to be the anonymous 'other disciple' of 1: 35–42 and
18: 15–16? He was clearly one of the inner three. Peter
is mentioned in the gospel by name, so it cannot be he.
James was martyred early (Acts 12: 2). Only John is
left. That the Baptist is designated in the gospel by a
simple 'John' without additional description is further
evidence that this is the author's name.

It is necessary, however, to add that this ascription
of the gospel and epistle to John the apostle is doubted
by many to-day. Beginning with the obvious difference
in the portrait and teaching of Jesus apparent between
the synoptic gospels and the fourth gospel, and noting
the hesitation which there seems to have been in the
second century A.D. to accept the apostolic authorship,
they attribute the gospel and epistles to another John.
Papias, living about the second quarter of the second
century, is quoted by Eusebius, the fourth-century
ecclesiastical historian, as saying that there were two
Johns in Ephesus, one of whom was the apostle, while
the other is styled 'the presbyter' or 'the elder'. The
passage is obscure, but Eusebius may be right in thus

interpreting Papias. Jerome was the first to suggest that this John the elder is the same as the author of the second and third epistles who does in fact describe himself by this title (2 Jn. 1 and 3 Jn. 1). The ascription of the gospel and the epistles to the presbyter John has gained wide credence to-day. On this view, the author distinguishes himself from 'the witness' of 19: 35 and 21: 24, who is the beloved disciple, and the book becomes the gospel of John the elder according to the witness of John the apostle.

The last word has clearly not yet been said or written on the vexed question of the authorship of the Johannine writings. It is by no means proved that Papias, of whose intelligence Eusebius in any case had a poor opinion, was distinguishing between two different Johns. He may have been referring to the same person. He gives the title 'elder' to all the apostles, and he calls John the elder 'a disciple of the Lord', a description at least vaguely reminiscent of 'the disciple whom Jesus loved'. Further, if the author of the Johannine epistles proves to be the apostle, it is no more unnatural that he should style himself an 'elder' (2 Jn. 1 and 3 Jn. 1) than that the apostle Peter should have done so (1 Pet. 5: 1).

Assuming then that the author of both gospel and epistles is none other than the apostle John, we know him as the son of a certain Zebedee, who was a master fisherman of Galilee. John and James, Simon and Andrew were fishing partners (Lk. 5: 10), and Zebedee was sufficiently well-to-do to employ hired servants (Mk. 1: 20). The family must have had good connexions in Jerusalem, as he was known to the high priest (18: 16), and the way in which Jesus commended His mother to John's care suggests that he even had a house in Jerusalem (19: 27). For an understanding of the distinctive message which the Holy Spirit prepared John to convey, there are two particular matters which call for elaboration. The first is the intimate relation in which he stood to the Lord Himself. Having been one of the Baptist's adherents, he was among the first to leave him and follow Him to whom the forerunner pointed (1: 35–40). Soon after, he became one of the permanent disciples (Mk. 1: 19–20) whom Jesus later named 'apostles' (Mk. 3: 13–17; Lk. 6: 12–14). More than that, he shared with his brother James and with Peter the privilege of forming an inner circle of intimates to whom the Master more freely disclosed His mind. It was Peter, James and John who were permitted to witness the raising of Jairus's daughter (Lk. 8: 51), see His glory on the Transfiguration mount (Mk. 9: 2), hear His apocalyptic teaching (Mk. 13: 3) and stay near Him during His bitter agony in the garden (Mk. 14: 33). If these were sacred experiences shared by the three, John appears to have been the most privileged of all. He was reclining next to Jesus in the upper room, and was so close to Him that he could lean back and whisper to Him without being overheard by the others (Jn. 13: 21–5; cf. 21: 20). This is the first occasion in the gospel on which the title 'disciple whom Jesus loved' is used, and it may well be that not until that sacred moment did John realize himself to be specially loved. The title is used again four times afterwards, and each time with the suggestion, faint or clear, of special privilege. It was to the beloved disciple, who had faithfully followed his Lord to His trial (18: 15–16) and to His cross, that He entrusted the care of His mother (19: 25–7). It was to the beloved disciple and to Peter that Mary Magdalene ran to bring the news of the empty sepulchre (20: 1–2). It was the beloved disciple who first recognized the risen Lord on the Galilean

shore and shouted to Peter: 'It is the Lord!' (21: 7) and
who shared in the private conversation which the Lord
had with Peter after breakfast (21: 20–3). It is John,
therefore, who was more qualified than any other one
of the twelve to convey to the Church the inner mind
of the Lord. It is appropriate that he should have written
what Clement of Alexandria called a 'spiritual gospel'.
He had enjoyed the most intimate possible relationship
with Jesus. He had seen Him with his eyes (1 Jn. 1: 1–3;
cf. 4: 14 and Jn. 1: 14); heard Him with his ears and
touched Him with his hands (1 Jn. 1: 1–3). He had
absorbed his Lord's own mind and could reflect His
secret thoughts. He had penetrated to the heart of His
self-revelation and had caught the spirit of his Master.

The second point to notice is that this holy fellowship
had profoundly influenced his character. John and
James, according to Mark, were nicknamed by Jesus
'Boanerges', which means 'sons of thunder' (Mk. 3: 17),
and there are several incidents in the gospel narratives
in which their stormy temperament appears. It is John
who resents and forbids the ministry of the exorcist who
was not one of the twelve (Lk. 9: 49–50). It was the
sons of thunder together who were offended by the
refusal of a Samaritan village to receive Jesus, and who
wanted like Elijah to call down fire from heaven to
consume it (Lk. 9: 51–6). And it was the same two
brothers who came with their mother to ask that the best
seats in the Kingdom might be reserved for them (Mk.
10: 35–45; Mt. 20: 20–8). How little they then seemed to
understand the spirit of Jesus! He had to rebuke them.
'You do not know what manner of spirit you are of', He
said (Lk. 9: 55). And again: 'You do not know what you
are asking' (Mt. 20: 22; Mk. 10: 38). It seems strange that
this son of thunder should have become known to us

as 'the apostle of love'. It is clear that the kindly sun of his Master's love had made the thunder-clouds evaporate. It was because he was 'the beloved disciple' that 'the son of thunder' became 'the apostle of love'.

The Holy Spirit had thus prepared the apostle John to hand down to posterity through his gospel and his epistles the predominant themes of his Lord's revelation. He desired to introduce his readers to the Person he had come to know and love. He wanted them to have fellowship with Him, too (1 Jn. 1: 3). He expected them to be transformed in character as he had been. In fact, he explains clearly the purposes for which he wrote. He wrote his gospel that his readers might believe in Him, and that believing they might have life (20: 31), and he wrote his first epistle to those who had believed, in order that they might know that they had life (1 Jn. 5: 13). Although his writings are perhaps the most philosophical in the New Testament, his ultimate purpose is seen to be practical. He desired his readers both to receive eternal life and to know that they had received it. For them to receive eternal life they must put their trust in Jesus Christ, since life resides in Him (1: 4). Therefore in his gospel he sets forth Jesus Christ in all His divine-human glory that men might see and believe. For his readers to know that they had received eternal life, it was necessary for them to understand clearly the indispensable marks of authentic Christianity. In his epistles, particularly in his first, he therefore proceeds to set these forth.

THE GOSPEL

The road to life is belief (3: 14–16, 36; 6: 47; 20: 31). But what is the road to belief? The clearest Biblical answer is given by St. Paul in Romans 10: 17: 'Faith

cometh by hearing, and hearing by the word of God.'
Faith is never isolated. It is always a response to God's
initiative. It is evoked by His word, or, as St. John would
have said, by His 'testimony'. Testimony leads to faith,
and faith to life. This is the principal thesis of St. John's
gospel. It is the gospel of testimony to Christ. It is the call
for belief on testimony. It is the offer of life on belief.
What testimony, therefore, does the apostle produce?

He begins with human testimony. In the opening
words of the gospel, as in those of the first epistle and
the Revelation, he bears his own apostolic witness to
the Lord Jesus Christ. It is noteworthy that he begins
his gospel with statement, not proof. As the book
Genesis is introduced by: 'In the beginning God',
affirming the Father's existence, so St. John's gospel is
introduced by 'In the beginning was the Word', affirming the Son's pre-existence. These eternal truths are a
fit subject for dogma, not for demonstration, because
they are the product of divine revelation, not of human
speculation. They are to be accepted or rejected on
testimony, for faith is not belief in spite of evidence but
belief on testimony. So the gospel begins, and ends
(19: 35; 21: 24), with apostolic testimony. In the inter-
vening chapters successive persons are brought before
Christ, and thus confronted by Him, bear witness to
Him. John the Baptist's is the most elaborate testimony
given (1: 7–8, 19–34; 3: 25–30; 10: 40–2), perhaps
because it was through him that the evangelist himself
had come to believe (1: 35–40). Andrew also had believed, and through his testimony Simon had come
(1: 40–2). Philip's witness brought Nathanael (1: 43–51),
and through the woman of Samaria many Samaritans
believed on Him (4: 39).

But Jesus did not rely on the testimony of men to

validate His claims (5: 33–5). Nor did He even rely on His own testimony. True, when the Samaritans came to Him they roundly declared that their faith now rested not on the woman's but on His own word (4: 39–42). Yet He said: 'If I bear witness to Myself, My witness is not true' (5: 31). To understand this statement it must be remembered that the reliability of a testimony depends on the authority of the witness. It is the person who guarantees the word. This being so, only a divine Person can authenticate divine claims. Therefore, for Christ to advance self-testimony only would be to beg the question. He would be assuming His divinity in order to establish it. Something greater was required, namely independent divine testimony.

It is precisely this kind of testimony which He claimed to possess. He depended, He said, primarily neither on human testimony (5: 34), nor on self-testimony (5: 31). 'There is another', He declared (5: 32), 'who bears witness to me, and I know that the testimony which He bears to me is true.' He was undoubtedly referring to the Father, who was continually bearing witness to the Son in His words, and in His works. Both the words and the works of Jesus are repeatedly said to be not the Son's testimony to Himself but the Father's testimony to the Son. The authority for the words and the power for the works came from the Father. Similarly, the Son does not 'glorify Himself', that is, manifest His divine Person. It is the Father who 'glorifies' the Son (8: 50, 54; 17: 1). Hence, on the two occasions recorded by St. John in which Jesus made an explicit claim to deity and as a result 'the Jews took up stones to stone Him' for blasphemy, He appealed to the Father's testimony to substantiate His claim (8: 48–59; 10: 24–39). This divine testimony is threefold:

(i) *The Father's word of testimony was written in the Old Testament Scriptures*. Jesus continually rebuked His contemporaries for refusing to believe in Him on the testimony of the Scriptures. 'Have you not read?' and 'did you never read?' are formulas which introduced several reproofs for failure to understand. His enemies mistook His person and His disciples misunderstood His work through ignorance of the Scriptures. The Scriptures embodied the Father's written testimony to the Son (5: 37–47; 10: 34–6; cf. Lk. 16: 29–31; 24: 25–7, 44–7).

(ii) *The Father's word of testimony was spoken through the lips of Jesus*. 'If you believe not his [Moses'] writings, how will you believe My words?' Both were the Father's testimony. If they did not accept the Father's testimony through the writings of Moses, they would not accept His testimony through the lips of Jesus. Yet this testimony could be relied upon as true because it was not His but His who sent Him, even though it was conveyed through His own lips. His self-testimony was 'true' or valid only because He knew Him from whom He had come and to whom He was going (8: 12–15). He spoke on the Father's authority, so that 'I and He who sent Me' (8: 16) bore a joint witness, and the law of Moses stated that the testimony of two was true (8: 17–18; cf. Deut. 19: 15). It is in this connexion that mention must be made of the characteristic designation of God in St. John's gospel as 'He who sent Me' (thirty-six times) and of Jesus as 'He whom He hath sent.' These paraphrases for the names 'Father' and 'Son' occur nearly always in contexts where the Son's authority is challenged or the Father's claimed. 'He who sent' vindicates the authority of 'Him whom He hath sent'. 'He whom God has sent utters the words of God' (3: 31–6). 'He who sent Me is true, and I declare to the world what I have heard from Him' (8: 25–30; cf. 7: 25–31). The validity of His testimony is due to His descent from heaven (3: 11–13).

So it is that again and again Jesus denies that He speaks His words on His own authority. His authority is derived from the Father who is their author. Is not He Himself the Word of God incarnate (1: 1, 14)? Then His words are the words of God (3: 34). 'My teaching is not Mine but His who sent Me' (7: 16–17). 'I do nothing on My own authority but speak thus as the Father taught Me' (8: 28). 'I have not spoken on My own authority; the Father who sent Me has Himself given Me commandment what to say and what to speak' (12: 49–50). 'I have given them the words which Thou gavest Me' (17: 8). 'I have given them Thy word' (17: 14). Christ expected everyone who heard Him to believe His words because they were God's words, and 'he who receives His testimony sets his seal to this, that God is true' (3: 33; cf. 1 Jn. 5: 9–10).

(iii) *The Father's word of testimony was dramatized in the works of Jesus.* In these works, similarly, Jesus is not advancing claims for Himself, since in the works as in the words it is the Father who speaks. Just as He could say: 'My teaching is not Mine but His who sent Me' (7: 16), He could also speak of 'the works which the Father has granted Me to accomplish' (5: 36; cf. 5: 19–31 and 10: 31–9). It is because the Father was in the Son and the Son in the Father that what the Son did He did 'from the Father' and what the Father did He did 'through the Son'. The works were the Father's, although performed through the Son. This double testimony of words and works should have been adequate to elicit faith (14: 8–11), and in fact many simple

I

folk saw the works (6: 14), heard the words (7: 40–1), and believed.

But in what sense were His works a testimony? How was His 'glory' manifested through them (2: 11)? St. John draws attention not to their miraculous character as 'wonders' but rather to their spiritual significance as 'signs'. In them the Father's claims concerning the Son were visibly set forth in such a way as both to command attention and to enlighten the understanding. Here is the Father 'glorifying' the Son. Nicodemus was quite right in declaring that such 'signs' were performed by Jesus only because God was with Him (3: 2). They proved that He was the Christ (7: 31; 9: 16; 11: 45–8). Because of them the crowds followed Him (6: 2), and 'many believed in His name' (2: 23). It is true that in two passages (4: 48 and 20: 24–9), as in several passages in the synoptic gospels, a craze for the seeing of 'signs' is deprecated, but what is condemned is a superstitious reverence for material miracles, not faith born of an intelligent understanding of signs. This is evident because John tells his readers that he had purposely made a selection of signs as a dramatic word of testimony through which they should believe (20: 30–1).

It is difficult to analyse St. John's gospel without resorting to an artificial arrangement, but the following signs appear to have been selected. Each is accompanied by one or more explanatory discourses, and can be associated directly or indirectly with an 'I am' verse, in which is crystallized the particular claim set forth in the sign.

(a) Jesus claims to inaugurate a new order, declaring 'I am He', viz., the Messiah (4: 26). The turning of the water into wine is said to be the first of His signs (2: 11). The symbolism is clear. The 'six stone jars . . . for Jewish rites of purification' (2: 6) stood for the law. It is through the miraculous intervention of Jesus that this water was replaced by the wine, which represented the gospel. Similarly, He cleansed the temple (centre of the worship of the Old Testament Church) and spoke of the temple which He would raise in its place. 'But He spoke of the temple of His body', comments the evangelist (2: 21), interpreting the words as referring not only to His resurrection body, but also to His mystical Body, the Church, which would be the new Temple (cf. Eph. 2: 21–2; 1 Cor. 3: 16; 2 Cor. 6: 16). To enter this new order, Jesus went on to explain to Nicodemus, a new birth was necessary (3: 1–15). The water of Jacob's well would give place to the 'water of life' (4: 1–15). The Samaritan woman evidently intended to receive the blessings of the New Covenant, for she 'left her water jar' (4: 28).

(*b*) Jesus claims to bestow new life, declaring: 'I am the Life' (11: 25; 14: 6). The discourse in which this claim is elaborated (5: 10–29) follows two signs in which it is exhibited. The first is the healing of the nobleman's son (4: 46–54), which is in fact called 'the second sign' (4: 54), and the other is the healing of the cripple at the pool of Bethesda (5: 1–9). In both these 'signs' the health of the body symbolizes the life of the soul. Eternal life begins now in this age, and is given in response to faith in Jesus Christ (5: 21–4). Judgment also begins now (5: 22–3; cf. 3: 16–21, 36), but both life and judgment will be brought to their consummation hereafter (5: 25–9).

(*c*) Jesus claims to satisfy the soul, declaring: 'I am the Bread of Life' (6: 35, 48, 51). The sign in this case is the feeding of the five thousand (6: 1–15), the only miracle recorded by all four evangelists. In the accompanying discourse (6: 25–65) it is made plain that He who fed the hungry multitudes can satisfy the starving soul. The bread which He will give for the life of the world is His flesh (6: 51). He is clearly referring to His cross. It is His torn flesh which is 'food indeed' and it is His shed blood which is 'drink indeed' (6: 55). Eternal life is one of the 'benefits of His passion'. Only through His death is life available for us. What, then, is the eating and drinking? It is faith, that is, personal acceptance of Christ and self-committal to Him, of which eating and drinking are a striking physical illustration. He could say with equal ease: 'He who believes has eternal life' (6: 47) and 'He who eats My flesh and drinks My blood has eternal life' (6: 54). As Augustine wrote: '*Crede et manducasti*', that is, 'Believe and thou hast eaten.' If this discourse is historical, it can hardly be said to have a direct reference to the Lord's Supper which had not yet been instituted. Many modern scholars are of the opinion, however, that St. John wrote his gospel against the background of the Church's liturgical services, and that he himself interpreted the discourse on the Bread of Life as referring to the Holy Communion. Certainly the Holy Communion service perpetuates the profound spiritual truth that eternal life depends on our believing appropriation of Christ crucified.

(*d*) Jesus claims to reveal God, declaring: 'I am the Light of the World' (8: 12; 9: 5). This section opens with the suggestion of His brothers that He should go to Judea to make Himself known (7: 1–3). 'If You do these things, show Yourself to the world', they said (7: 4–5). But Jesus waited until His time had come, and then, after going up secretly, suddenly in the middle of the feast appeared in the Temple (7: 6–14). Then after speaking to the Pharisees about His word which would reveal to them the truth (8: 31–2; cf. 14: 6; 17: 6, 17;

18: 37), He performed the sign of healing the man born blind (ch. 9). The One who restored physical sight did so on God's authority as the Sent One, whose very title is symbolically found in the name of the pool 'Siloam' (9: 7), through whose waters the man had been enabled to see. They who follow Him shall not walk in darkness, but shall have the light of life (8: 12).

(*e*) Jesus claims to forgive sins, declaring, 'I am the Good Shepherd' (10: 11, 14), 'I am the Door' (10: 7, 9) and 'I am the Way' (14: 6). It is perhaps not fanciful to see the sign to which the Good Shepherd discourse is to be annexed in the whole story of the Passion (chs. 13–19), culminating in the flow of blood and water which John witnessed and to which he evidently attached great symbolical meaning (19: 34–5). Here we see the Shepherd laying down His life for His sheep, and claiming that through death His sheep may live (10: 10, 11, 15, 17–18). The grain of wheat falls into the ground and dies, that a harvest may be assured (12: 24, 32–3). That the cross is the supreme 'sign' is clear from even a cursory reading of the gospel. It is there that Jesus was 'lifted up' (3: 14–15; 8: 28; 12: 32–3), not only physically, but spiritually as a magnet to draw all men to Himself. It is there, too, that He was supremely 'glorified', that is, revealed in the full beauty of His divine nature (7: 39; 12: 16, 23, 28; 13: 31–2; 17: 1–5).

(*f*) Jesus claims to overcome death, declaring: 'I am the Resurrection' (11: 25). His glorification was completed not in His death, but in His triumph over death (11: 4, 40). The sign which demonstrated this was the raising of Lazarus (ch. 11), which was intended, like the other signs, to evoke faith (11: 15). It succeeded in doing so (12: 9–11, 17–19). But this final sign was an anticipation of the greater sign of Christ's own Resurrection. John himself knew the efficacy of this sign, for he wrote of himself (20: 8) that 'he saw and believed'. Not only the empty tomb and the undisturbed grave-clothes but the risen Jesus Himself constituted the sign. At His first general appearance to the ten 'He showed them His hands and His side' (20: 20). Thomas refused to believe until he had seen the same sign (20: 25), but, seeing it, confessed 'my Lord and my God' (20: 28–9).

Such is the comprehensive testimony borne to us by the Father concerning the Son. St. John records it with diligence, jealous for the honour of his Lord, resolved that his readers should themselves believe in Him, and, believing, should receive life in His name.

THE EPISTLES

But the Apostle is not satisfied that we should receive life. It is his further purpose that we should know that we have received it. Clearly one cannot enjoy a gift unless one knows that one possesses it. Therefore, if God means us to receive and enjoy eternal life (6: 40), He must mean us to know we possess it. So St. John wrote his first epistle to those who had believed that they might know they had eternal life (5: 13). He was impelled to enlarge on this theme by the circumstances of his own church. The Ephesian church was evidently being deeply disturbed by false teaching of a particularly dangerous kind. The heretical teachers are 'antichrists' (2: 18) and 'liars' (2: 22), 'deceivers' (2: 26; 2 Jn. 7) and 'false prophets' (4: 1). He wanted both to expose their hypocrisy and to confirm the faith of the true believers. The heresy appears to have been a kind of incipient Gnosticism, very similar to, if not identical with, that taught by one Cerinthus, who is known to have been an opponent of St. John's in Ephesus. There were three particular aspects of this poisonous teaching. Firstly, they claimed to 'have the Father' (2: 22–3; 2 Jn. 9), but denied the Son. They probably taught that Jesus of Nazareth was a mere man, the natural child of Joseph and Mary. Any idea of an incarnation was impossible to them, because they regarded matter as essentially evil. Upon this man at his baptism 'the Spirit' or 'the Christ' descended, and from him before the cross 'the Spirit' or 'the Christ' flew back to heaven. This rubbish was a denial of both the Incarnation and the Atonement. It robbed Christ's person of divinity, His teaching of authority and His death of efficacy. The beloved disciple is indignant at this insult to his divine Lord, the Word made flesh. He affirms in the strongest possible terms that anyone who denies that Jesus is 'the Christ come in the flesh' is a liar and the antichrist (2: 22; 4: 1–3; 2 Jn. 7), and that no one who rejects the Son can possess the Father (2: 23–4). Jesus the Christ, the Son of God, is 'He who came by water and blood' (5: 6). This is an obscure phrase, but may well refer to His baptism and His cross, both of which John declares, in opposition to the heretical teaching, were experiences through which the divine-human Jesus of Nazareth passed.

The heretics were mistaken in ethics as well as in doctrine, and probably for the same basic reason. If matter is essentially evil, not only is an incarnation impossible, but the human body is a mere envelope for the spirit, and morality becomes a subject of indifference. Nothing which the body does can harm the spirit within. It is possible, they perhaps argued, to 'be righteous' without 'doing righteousness'. This second error John strenuously denies. His defence of the truth is vigorous. 'He who says: "I know Him" but disobeys His commandments is a liar' (2: 4–5). The love of the Father and the love of the world are incompatible (2: 15–17). The child of God must 'purify himself even as He is pure' (3: 3). 'Little children, let no one deceive you. He who does right is righteous, as He is righteous' (3: 7; 3 Jn. 11). There follow the difficult sentences which suggest that sin is an impossibility for the true Christian. 'No one born of God commits sin; for God's nature abides in him, and he cannot sin because he is born of God' (3: 9). John cannot, however, be teaching the impossibility of sinning because he has stated in 2: 1 that there is a provision of forgiveness—'if any man sins'. He is probably referring rather to the regular habit of sin, 'No one born of God practises sin', and he uses a present infinitive in the phrase 'he is not able to sin' which could be translated 'he is not able to go on sinning'. In all this John is simply echoing his Master's teaching and recalling his Master's example. Three years' intimacy with Him had convinced him that Jesus was unique and sinless (1 Jn. 3: 5; cf. Jn. 8: 46). The Jesus who exposed the Samaritan woman's immoral life (Jn. 4: 16–18), told even righteous Nicodemus that he needed to be born again (3: 1–15), warned the cripple to sin no more (5: 14), cleansed the Temple of its greedy traffickers (2: 13–17), told the Pharisees that they were mere slaves of sin (8: 31–2), urged His disciples to keep His commandments (14: 15, 21–4; 15: 14) and prayed that the Father would keep and sanctify His own (17: 11–17), was the Holy One who required truth in the inward parts. 'Little children, keep yourselves from idols' (1 Jn. 5: 21) was John's last word to them.

The third aspect of the heretics' system which received the Apostle's condemnation was their superior attitude to others. They were religious snobs, claiming to have a special revelation of their own. They were the 'spiritual' ones, the enlightened aristocracy, the religious *élite*. They despised the rest. John flatly contradicts their claim. Writing to the whole church, he says: 'You have been anointed by the Holy One, and you all know' (Jn. 2: 20). There is no esoteric revelation. The apostolic teaching is the possession of the whole Church (2: 27). Besides, members of the Church must love one another (2 Jn. 5). They are brethren. It was the Lord's last prayer that His disciples should be one (Jn. 17: 20–3). No man can be 'in the light' if he hates his brother (1 Jn. 2: 9–11). The beloved disciple remembers how his Lord humbled Himself to wash His disciples' feet (Jn. 13: 1–11), and how He told them to wash one another's feet (13: 12–17). This was His new commandment, that they should love one another (13: 34–5). He laid down His life for His friends (15: 12–13, 17). So 'we ought to lay down our lives for the brethren' (1 Jn. 3: 16). All our love is but a response to His. The beloved disciple knew this from his own experience. The way to love is to be loved. 'Herein is love, not that we loved God but that He loved us . . .' (4: 10.) 'We love, because He first loved us' (4: 19). God has manifested His love by giving His Son (4: 9, 10, 14). We must manifest ours also in sacrifice (3: 16–18). 'He who does not love does not know God; for God is love' (4: 8).

This then is the threefold test of authentic Christianity. John writes to undermine the false assurance of counterfeit Christians and to buttress the right assurance of real Christians. He hits hard at mere professors of religion. Like James, he draws a contrast between what a man claims to be and what he really is. 'If we say we have fellowship with Him while we walk in darkness we lie . . . If we say we have no sin we deceive ourselves . . . If we say we have not sinned we make Him a liar

. . . '(1: 6, 8, 10). 'He who says "I know Him" . . . He who says he abides in Him . . . He who says he is in the light . . .' (2: 4, 6, 9) must manifest his declaration in a life of obedience and love. In contrast to these empty boasts, John gives expression to the Christian's sure convictions. Often he uses the phrase 'hereby we know', and the tests of assurance are the same. 'By this you know the Spirit of God: every spirit which confesses that Jesus Christ has come in the flesh is of God' (4: 2). This is the test of belief. 'By this we may be sure that we know Him, if we keep His commandments' (2: 3). This is the test of obedience. 'We know that we have passed out of death into life, because we love the brethren' (3: 14). This is the test of love. He makes the same affirmations negatively. The professor who fails to pass these tests is a liar, and his hypocrisy must be exposed. 'Who is the liar but he who denies that Jesus is the Christ?' (2: 22). 'If we say we have fellowship with Him while we walk in darkness, we lie . . .' (1: 6). 'If anyone says: "I love God", and hates his brother, he is a liar' (4: 20).

These are the three proofs of genuine Christianity. John brings them all together at the beginning of his fifth chapter. 'Everyone who believes that Jesus is the Christ is a child of God, and everyone who loves the Parent loves the child. By this we know that we love the children of God, when we love God and obey His commandments' (5: 1–5). Unless the professing Christian is characterized by right belief, godly obedience and brotherly love, he is a counterfeit. He cannot have been born again, for he who is 'born of God' is one who believes (5: 1) and obeys (3: 9) and loves (4: 7).

So John lays down his pen. He has put the enemies

of the gospel to flight. 'They went out from us, but they were not of us; for if they had been of us, they would have continued with us; but they went out, that it might be made plain that they all are not of us' (2: 19). The humble, true believer, on the other hand, possesses life, and is assured of his new birth, not only because he manifests the qualities of the new life which John has elaborated, but because he possesses Christ Himself, and he has the sure testimony of God that 'he who has the Son has the life' (5: 9–12).

Chapter VII

THE MESSAGE OF PETER

The sufferings of Christ and the subsequent glory.
1 Peter 1: 11

*Rejoice in so far as you share Christ's sufferings, that
you may also rejoice and be glad when His glory is
revealed.*—1 Peter 4: 13

IT is St. Paul who tells us that the three pre-eminent
Christian graces are faith, hope and love (1 Cor. 13:
13). If he is himself the apostle of faith, and St. John is
the apostle of love, St. Peter is the apostle of hope. No
doubt this is an over-simplification. The first epistle of
Peter has a wider message still. It is 'a microcosm of
Christian faith and duty, the model of a pastoral charge,
composed of diverse materials and of many themes'.[1]
Nevertheless, the emphasis is upon the Christian's
'hope', whose object is so glorious and certain that he
can endure suffering with patience and fortitude. Like
his Master before him, the Christian must suffer before
entering into his glory.

The first epistle of Peter has been accepted as authentic from the earliest days, and figures in the list
which Eusebius gives of New Testament works which
are beyond dispute. Its Petrine authorship has, however,
been doubted by some in recent years, largely on account
of its excellent Greek style which, it is argued, could
hardly be supposed to have come from a rough Galilean

[1] *The First Epistle of St. Peter*, by E. G. Selwyn, p. 1. (Macmillan,
1946.)

fisherman. The fine literary qualities of the epistle can best be explained by supposing that Silvanus, who is mentioned in 5: 12, was more than a mere stenographer. Peter says indeed that he 'wrote through Silvanus', for whose Christian character he had a high regard, and it may well be that Silvanus had a share in the composition of the epistle. He was evidently quite a prominent figure in the early Church, having accompanied Paul on part of his second missionary journey (Acts 15: 40; 16: 19, 25; 17: 4, 10, 14; 18: 5), and being a 'prophet' (Acts 15: 32). He was also associated with Paul and Timothy in the writing of the letters to the Thessalonians (1 Thess. 1: 1; 2 Thess. 1: 1). At the same time, Peter does not include Silvanus's name in his greeting (1: 1). He writes in his own name, on his own authority (e.g., 5: 1). Further, there are a number of features in the epistle itself which suggests Peter's personal reminiscences. He had had a vivid experience of the 'living hope' which floods into the soul 'through the resurrection of Jesus Christ from the dead' (1 Pet. 1: 3); he had been 'a witness of the sufferings of Christ' (5:1) and could recall His buffeting (2: 20) and His silence before His tormentors (2: 22–3); he could never forget the Shepherd's thrice-repeated command to tend His flock (5: 2; Jn. 21: 15–17). Silvanus may therefore have been responsible for the style, but the letter is Peter's.

More serious doubts have from the earliest times surrounded the authorship of the second epistle. It certainly purports to come from Peter's hand (1: 1) and seems to refer to the first epistle (3: 1), but the style is more abrupt and complicated, and critics have wondered whether in Peter's lifetime Paul's epistles could have been ranked with the sacred Scriptures of the Old Testament (3: 15–16). These and other arguments are serious, but they are not conclusive. It is at least possible that if the polished style of the first epistle is due to Silas's composition, the rugged Greek of the second is due to the apostle's own dictation or to the use of an inferior amanuensis. Also, full weight should be given to the author's claim to have been present on the Transfiguration Mount (1: 16–18), to have received from the lips of Jesus a prophecy about his death (1: 13–14; cf. Jn. 21: 18–19), and to have been acquainted with Paul (3: 15–16).

Simon Peter is perhaps the most attractive of all the apostolic writers of the New Testament. He figures prominently in the gospel narratives and in the early part of the Acts, and his natural human frailty endears him to the Christian reader. Like his brother Andrew, Simon was by trade a fisherman. They were partners with that other pair of brothers, John and James, the sons of Zebedee (Lk. 5: 10). They hailed originally from Bethsaida, on the northern shore of the Sea of Galilee (Jn. 1: 44), but Simon later had his home in Capernaum (Mk. 1: 21, 29) on the lake's north-westerly shore, where he lived with his wife, his mother-in-law and Andrew (Mk. 1: 29–30; cf. 1 Cor. 9: 5).

It is not difficult to imagine Simon's temperament in those early days. He was a hot-headed northerner with a turbulent disposition. The storms which tossed his fishing bark on the Lake of Galilee were reflected in those which raged in his own soul. He was as impetuous as the waves, as impulsive as the wind. Jesus detected at once his principal weakness of character, and prophesied that although he was now as shifting as the sands he would become as solid and dependable as the rock (Jn. 1: 42; cf. Mt. 16: 18). Becoming first a disciple (Mk. 1: 16–18) and then an apostle (Lk. 6: 13–14), <u>Peter quickly</u>

became the accepted leader of the apostolic band. In every list both of the Twelve and of the Three he is named first, and he assumed the role of spokesman for the others. His leadership continues into the early chapters of the Acts.

But there is more to be said. Simon was a Galilean, and Galilee was a hotbed of Messianic hopes. The simple peasants clung doggedly to the prophetic utterances which promised the reversal of Israel's fortunes and the establishment of God's Kingdom. They hated their Roman overlords, and longed for the day when the Messiah would bring the Roman occupation of Palestine to an end. It is almost certain that Simon shared these revolutionary sentiments. Temperament and environment combined to make him one of those Jews who were eagerly awaiting 'the redemption of Jerusalem' (Lk. 2: 38), 'the consolation of Israel' (Lk. 2: 25) and 'the Kingdom of God' (Mk. 15: 43). This was the hope which glowed in his soul.

It is not surprising, therefore, that when news reached him that a prophet had come from the wilderness to announce the Messiah's approach, Simon left his fishing and went south to hear him. He evidently accepted John's teaching, was baptized by him, and became his disciple. His brother Andrew was present on the occasion when the Baptist saw Jesus and pointed to Him as 'the Lamb of God' (Jn. 1: 35–40). Andrew left the Baptist, followed Jesus, and then went to fetch Simon with the thrilling words: 'We have found the Messiah' (Jn. 1: 41–2). This was Simon's first introduction to the One who was to become the object of all his hopes. He accompanied Him, heard Him, watched Him, and wondered at Him. Gradually the fiery hope which had smouldered in his heart since boyhood began to glow, until at Cæsarea Philippi, among the hills at the foot of Mount Hermon, it burst into flame with his great confession of faith: 'Thou art the Christ, the Son of the Living God' (Mt. 16: 13–16). His hope was realized. This was the supreme moment of his lifetime. The Messiah had come. Jesus accepted the designation, told Peter that the Father had revealed this truth to him, forbade the disciples to tell anyone that He was the Christ (Mt. 16: 20) and began at once to teach them 'that the Son of man must suffer many things' (Mt: 16: 21; Mk. 8: 31). They had acknowledged His person; they must now discover His work. They had grasped the fact of His Kingdom; they must now learn its character. He had not come to drive the legions of Rome out of the Promised Land. He had come to die for the sins of the world. The way to His throne was the steep, rugged ascent of Calvary. He must suffer before He could enter into His glory. The price of His crown was a cross. Simon listened aghast. His triumph was short-lived. The Messiah could not be killed. He had come to reign, not to die. He was destined for glory, not for suffering. So he blurted out: 'God forbid, Lord! This shall never happen to you' (Mt. 16: 22). Jesus turned and rebuked him, 'Get thee behind Me, Satan! You are a stumbling-block to Me; for you are not on the side of God, but of men' (Mt. 16: 23). The Apostle who had just been the recipient of the Father's revelation had become the object of the devil's deception.

Only a week later Jesus took Peter, James and John up the mountain and was transfigured before their eyes. It was a foretaste of His glory, in fulfilment of His promise that some of them would not taste of death until they had seen 'the Kingdom of God come with power' (Mk. 9: 1). Peter saw 'His majesty . . . on the holy

mountain' (2 Pet. 1: 16–18). But he could not understand and would not revise his prejudices. Gradually the
crisis drew near. In the upper room he saw the Lord
rise from supper, gird Himself with a towel and begin
to wash His disciples' feet. Peter at first refused to let
Jesus wash his feet (Jn. 13: 6–8). Had the Messiah come
to do a slave's work? In the garden he drew his sword,
lunged out in the darkness and slashed off the ear of
Malchus, the high priest's servant (Jn. 18: 10). He could
not let the King be arrested without a fight. He followed
Him into the city, albeit 'afar off' (Mk. 14: 54). The
Master's fearful predictions were coming true. Had he
been mistaken? Was this, then, not the Messiah after
all? He had boasted that he would be prepared even to
die for Him (Mk. 14: 31), but how could he give his
allegiance to a King who was being rejected by His own
nation? The final test came, and he denied Him, not
once but thrice. And he went out into the night to weep
bitterly, tears not just of remorse but of cruel disillusion-
ment. No doubt he followed the crowds up to Golgotha.
He saw the end. The hope he had nourished was extinguished. His heart was chilled. The Messiah was dead.

It is hard to imagine the two days of hell through
which Simon Peter passed. It is harder still to conceive
the overwhelming excitement of Easter Day. He ran to
the sepulchre with John (Jn. 20: 1–10). The tomb was
empty. The body had gone. And then he met the Lord
(1 Cor. 15: 5). It was a private interview. We do not
know what transpired. But we do know that Simon
Peter was 'born again unto a living hope by the resurrection of Jesus Christ from the dead' (1 Pet. 1: 3). We
also know that on the evening of the first Easter Day
the Lord appeared to the Ten in the upper room where
they were assembled and repeated what He had said to

K

the two disciples on the road to Emmaus. He had ex-
postulated with them: 'O fools, and slow of heart to
believe all that the prophets have spoken! Was it not
necessary that the Christ should suffer these things and
enter into His glory?' (Lk. 24: 25–6). Similarly, He
opened the minds of the Ten to understand the Scriptures and said to them: 'Thus it is written, that the
Christ should suffer and on the third day rise from the
dead, and that repentance and forgiveness of sins should
be preached in His name to all nations, beginning from
Jerusalem . . .' (Lk. 24: 44–7). Hope was reborn in
Peter's heart. The Christ had suffered for sins. He had
risen again, and would return in final glory.

That Peter had assimilated this message is clear from
his sermons in the early chapters of the Acts. The burden
of the primitive apostolic message was: 'You killed Him
. . . but God raised Him . . . and we are witnesses.'
Peter is no longer ashamed of the sufferings of the
Christ, for although they were caused by 'the hands of
lawless men', they were also part of 'the definite plan
and foreknowledge of God' (Acts 2: 23). What God
has 'foretold by the mouth of all the prophets, that His
Christ should suffer', He has fulfilled (Acts 3: 18). But
now He has been raised and exalted to be both 'a Prince
and a Saviour' (Acts 5: 31). Through Him there is forgiveness to all who repent and believe (Acts 2: 38; 3: 19;
4: 11–12; 5: 31; 10: 43). He will return both for the
'refreshing' of His people (3: 19–21) and for the judgment of the world (10: 42). Meanwhile, the disciples of
Jesus must wait patiently. There is no need to fight or
to intrigue. The impulsive apostle who first defended,
and then denied, his Lord now stands undaunted before the Sanhedrin, and submits humbly to cross-
examination. He is flogged and imprisoned. He sleeps

on the eve of expected execution (12: 6), and, if tradition is to be believed (cf. Jn. 21: 18–19), he finally died his Master's death, being crucified in Rome during the Neronian persecution. Where is the old fiery fighting spirit of Simon? It has been replaced by a new and living hope. The Christ had to suffer before entering into His glory. The Christian, too, must suffer if he is to share in the glory of Christ when it is finally revealed.

This is the exalted theme of Peter's letters. It will be seen how the Apostle was prepared by the Holy Spirit to teach it. The lesson he was slow to learn under the tutelage of Jesus he not only grasped after the Resurrection, but himself both proclaimed in his sermons and experienced in his life after the Ascension. He was qualified to go on teaching it. Moreover, he needed to. The Christians 'of the dispersion' (1 Pet. 1: 1) in the five provinces of Asia Minor to whom he wrote were evidently exposed to persecution. It was perhaps not the official execution of an imperial edict, for Peter urges his readers to submit to the Emperor and the local administration (2: 13–17), but it was severe enough to be termed a 'fiery ordeal' (4: 2) and was widespread (5: 9). Further, Peter writes to them from 'Babylon' (5: 13), an eloquent pseudonym for Rome, the centre of opposition to God. Perhaps the storm-clouds of more serious persecution were darkening the horizon. Ominous rumblings were already being heard. Local outbursts had begun. How should the Christians behave in such circumstances? What is the Christian attitude to undeserved suffering? These are the practical questions which face the Church of all ages, and which Peter had been specially equipped by the Holy Spirit to answer.

He turns the attention of his readers away from themselves to Christ. He reminds them that Christ suffered.

Seven times in his first epistle he uses the words 'suffer' and 'suffering' in reference to Christ (1: 11; 2: 21, 23; 3: 18; 4: 1, 13; 5: 1), and appears to glory in what once caused him shame and grief. There was purpose in His death. It was not a ghastly accident. It was not a tragic end to a promising life. He 'suffered for sins, the just for the unjust, that He might bring us to God' (3: 18). The great object of His sufferings was the bringing of sinners to God. So He suffered for their sins, He, the righteous, for them, the unrighteous. And He did it 'once'—not 'once upon a time' but 'once for all'. There was a completed achievement in His death. Again: 'He Himself bore our sins in His body on the tree' (2: 24). He died not just as our example (2: 21), but as our sin-bearer. The phrase 'to bear sin' recalls the Levitical sin-offering and the ritual of the scapegoat on the Day of Atonement, as has already been seen, but it also recalls the fifty-third chapter of the prophecy of Isaiah. Peter must have known that Jesus had applied the prophecy to Himself and had interpreted His death in the light of its teaching. In this passage therefore the Apostle uses five phrases reminiscent of Isaiah 53.

1 Peter 2	Isaiah 53
v. 22 No guile was found on His lips	v. 9 There was no deceit in His mouth
v. 23 He was reviled	v. 3 He was despised and rejected
v. 24 He Himself bore our sins	v. 12 He bore the sin of many
v. 24 By His wounds you have been healed	v. 5 With His stripes we are healed
v. 25 You were straying like sheep	v. 6 All we like sheep have gone astray

Jesus, the suffering servant of the Lord, bore our sins,

was wounded for our transgression and bruised for our iniquities.

There is one other passage in his first epistle in which Peter refers to the cross. He is urging his readers to conduct themselves with humble reverence before God, and goes on to give his reason: 'You know that you were ransomed from the futile ways inherited from your fathers . . . with the precious blood of Christ, like that of a lamb without blemish or spot' (1: 18–19). The mention of an unblemished lamb in connexion with redemption makes it clear that Peter is referring to the Passover. It was through the shedding and sprinkling of the blood of the physically perfect Paschal lamb that the Israelites were rescued from slavery in Egypt, and it was through the shedding of the precious blood of Christ in all His moral perfection that they had been redeemed from the worse thraldom of 'the traditions of Gentile paganism'.[1] Further, it is not enough for the blood to have been shed. It needed to be sprinkled (1: 2), that is, applied to the individual sinner.

The purpose of Christ's sufferings is thus made clear, and it was through those sufferings that He entered His glory. God 'raised Him from the dead and gave Him glory' (1: 21). 'The sufferings of Christ and the subsequent glory', a phrase strongly reminiscent of the Lord's own words in Luke 24: 25–6, had been predicted by the prophets, although they did not fully understand to what they were referring. The Christ who was 'put to death as to flesh' was 'quickened as to spirit' (3: 18). He who suffered for sins once for all (3: 18) has now 'gone into heaven and is at the right hand of God, with angels, authorities, and powers subject to Him' (3: 22).

Now St. Peter's great theme is that the disciple is not

[1] Selwyn, op. cit. ad loc.

above his master, and that what happened to Christ will inevitably happen to the Christian. This applies to suffering, but it applies to glory also. First, he emphasizes the certainty that Christians will suffer. If he uses the words 'suffer' and 'suffering' seven times with reference to Christ, he uses them nine times with reference to Christians (2: 19, 20; 3: 14, 17; 4: 1, 15, 19; 5: 9, 10). 'The same experience of suffering is required of your brotherhood throughout the world' (5: 9). All Christians are called upon to suffer. 'To this you have been called, because Christ also suffered for you, leaving you an example' (2: 21). 'Beloved, do not be surprised at the fiery ordeal which comes upon you to prove you, as though something strange were happening to you' (4: 12). It is not 'strange' or 'surprising' at all. It is to be expected that the Christian will 'share Christ's sufferings'. He should 'rejoice' that it is so (4: 13). Had not Christ warned His followers of the world's hatred (Jn. 15: 18–25)? He had even gone so far as to pronounce a 'woe' upon His followers if all men were speaking well of them (Lk. 6: 26) and a blessing on those who were being 'persecuted for righteousness' sake' (Mt. 5: 10–12). St. Paul had warned his converts that it was only 'through many tribulations' that 'we must enter the Kingdom of God' (Acts 14: 22) and had told his Philippian friends that God gives His children the two privileges both of believing in Christ and of suffering for His sake (Phil. 1: 29).

Peter is not satisfied with a mere statement that suffering is inevitable for the Christian. He goes on to give his readers some very practical advice about how to behave when persecuted. Again, he points them to Christ. Not only will they suffer as Christ suffered, but they must learn to endure suffering as He endured it.

They are to submit patiently, and they are to make sure that they give no cause to the enemies of God to blaspheme. Outsiders will then see their good conduct and glorify God (1 Pet. 2: 12). They must 'be subject for the Lord's sake to every human institution' (2: 13), 'for it is God's will that by doing right' they should 'put to silence the ignorance of foolish men' (2: 15). So much for the duties of citizens. What about Christian slaves in pagan households? What if their master is cruel and punishes them unjustly? Peter's answer is clear. They must be 'submissive . . . with all respect, not only to the kind and gentle but also to the overbearing' (2: 18). It is no credit to be patient in bearing a punishment one has deserved, but if one is unfairly punished and takes it patiently, this has 'God's approval' (2: 19–20). In a word, we are to think of Christ. He has left us an 'example'. This particular word is unique in the Greek New Testament, and means a teacher's copybook alphabet. If we are to learn the A B C of Christian love and forbearance, we must trace out our lives on the pattern of His. We are to 'follow in His steps'. The words are eloquent coming from the pen of Peter who had said: 'I will follow Thee to prison and to death' (Lk. 22: 33) but in the event had only 'followed afar off'. Later, on the shore of Galilee, he had heard again the Master's command 'follow Me' (Jn. 21: 19), and this counsel he passes on to his readers. They are to follow in the steps of Jesus. 'When He was reviled, He did not revile in return; when He suffered, He did not threaten' (2: 23). This duty of humble submission rests not only on the citizen and on the slave but on the wife (3: 1–7). If she is married to an unbelieving husband, he 'may be won without a word by the behaviour of' his wife.

However much the Christian is called upon to suffer,

in public life or in the privacy of his own home, let him not fear. Let him humble himself under God's mighty hand, that in due time He may exalt him. Let him cast all his anxieties upon God, for He cares for him (5: 6–7). 'The Lord knows how to rescue the godly from trial' (2 Pet. 2: 9). The believer is 'elect according to the foreknowledge of God the Father, through sanctification of the Spirit unto obedience and sprinkling of the blood of Jesus Christ' (1 Pet. 1: 2), and in the purpose of this Blessed Trinity he is eternally secure. Besides, God is working out His purpose for His Church. He is building it upon Jesus Christ, the 'corner stone chosen and precious' which He has laid in Zion (2: 6). The Jewish builders have rejected it, but God has made it 'the head of the corner' (2: 7). Coming to Jesus, to 'that living stone, rejected by men but in God's sight chosen and precious', we ourselves 'like living stones' are being 'built into a spiritual house' (2: 4-5). The Church, thus constituted, is not only like a building. It is the new Israel, God's own possession, 'a holy priesthood' to offer to God the spiritual sacrifices of worship (2: 5), and 'a chosen race, a royal priesthood, a holy nation, God's own people' in order to 'declare the wonderful deeds of Him' who has called us 'out of darkness into His marvellous light' (2: 9). Peter here takes some of the epithets by which the old Israel is described in Exodus 19: 5–6, and transfers them to the new Israel, the Christian Church. The building is secure because God is constructing it. The nation is safe because God has chosen it. Christians need not be afraid. Those called upon to suffer can confidently 'entrust their souls to a faithful creator' (4: 19).

Not only can they put faith in God now, but they can hope in God for the future also. Both our 'faith and hope are in God' (1: 21). The reason is this. If we share Christ's sufferings (4: 13), we shall certainly share His glory (5: 1). This is the Christian's double 'koinonia', or 'fellowship'. We may 'for a little while . . . have to suffer various trials' (1: 6), but such tribulation tests, strengthens and purifies our faith as fire does gold (1: 7), and we can rejoice now in the 'inheritance' which will be ours one day. It is absolutely certain. It is 'imperishable, undefiled and unfading', and it is 'reserved in heaven for us' (1: 4). This is our 'living hope'—'living' because it is 'never extinguished by untoward circumstances'.[1] It is not a vague, irrational sentiment. It is centred on Christ and it is anchored to history. It was created by the resurrection of Christ (1: 3) and it will be realized at the return of Christ (1: 7). When He is 'revealed' (1: 7), our final salvation will also be 'revealed' (1: 5). Meanwhile, we are 'guarded by God's power through faith' (1: 5), and until Christ is revealed to our sight we can believe and love Him who is invisible and can rejoice with unutterable joy (1: 8). 'Therefore,' writes Peter, 'gird up your minds, be sober, set your hope fully upon the grace that is coming to you at the revelation of Jesus Christ' (1: 13).

This link between the warning of present sufferings and the promise of future glory recurs several times in the epistle. It is even possible that the phrase in 1: 11 already quoted, 'the sufferings of Christ and the subsequent glory', refers not to Christ but to the Christian. The phrase could (perhaps more accurately) be translated 'the sufferings of the Christward road'[2], sufferings endured, that is, not by Christ but for Christ. The 'prophets' will then be Christian, not Hebrew.

---

[1] Selwyn, op. cit. ad loc.
[2] ibid.

In 3: 8–18 Peter repeats his teaching that the Christian must not retaliate, even if he is innocent. Indeed, so far from seeking his revenge upon his enemies, he must desire their blessing (3: 8–14). He goes on to give them advice about what they must do in a time of persecution. They must 'reverence Christ as Lord', committing the situation to His sovereign control; they must 'always be prepared to make a defence' to anyone who questions them concerning 'the hope that is in' them (3: 15), so long as they do it with humility; and they must be sure to keep their own conscience clear (3: 16–18). The hope which burns brightly in them should attract the attention of others. The world has nothing like this.

Similarly, if we rejoice in so far as we 'share Christ's sufferings', we shall 'rejoice and be glad when His glory is revealed' (4: 13). We must not suffer as evildoers (4: 15), but if we 'are reproached for the name of Christ' and suffer as Christians, 'the spirit of glory and of God' rests upon us (4: 14, 16). This phrase is a little obscure, but the general meaning is clear. The 'glory', which is God's manifested presence and which is not yet fully revealed (v. 13), yet rests already in measure upon the suffering Christian, a foretaste of the coming bliss.

The sufferings and the glory are therefore to be as characteristic of the Christian as they were of the Christ. All his life is to be coloured by his present experience and his future expectation. The elders are to tend the flock willingly and eagerly, not as domineering over them but as examples to them, knowing that when the Chief Shepherd appears they will obtain 'the unfading crown of glory' (5: 1–4). So, too, the younger ones are to be humble, sober, and watchful (5: 5–11). Temptations as well as trials are to be endured in the light of the coming glory. Perhaps the best exposition of this

more general theme is the third chapter of the second
epistle. Here Peter first argues with scoffers the certainty
of Christ's return (3–7), and then explains to sinners its
delay (8–10). It is due not to God's sloth, but to His
mercy. He prolongs the day of grace because He is not
willing that any should perish. Nevertheless, the day
will come as unexpectedly as a burglar. And what are
the practical implications for daily Christian living of
'the coming of the day of God' (12)? Peter's answer is
that as the Lord's return will usher in 'new heavens and
a new earth', the characteristics of the life we shall live
then should govern our present earthly pilgrimage.
'What sort of persons ought you to be?' (11). What
should be the marks of our Christian behaviour?

(*a*) *Holiness.* This world is sin-stained. But it will be
dissolved. Righteousness will dwell in the new universe
(13). Therefore we must live lives of 'holiness and godliness' now (12). The need for righteous conduct is
stressed many times in Peter's letters. As obedient
children, we are to be holy as God is holy (1 Pet. 1:
14–16). As 'aliens and exiles' (1 Pet. 2: 11; cf. 1: 1) on
this earth, possessing primarily a heavenly citizenship,
we must 'abstain from the passions of the flesh that wage
war against the soul'. Our very sufferings help to wean
us from the world and to fashion our lives not according
to our human passions but according to God's will
(1 Pet. 4: 1–7). We must show our knowledge by our
behaviour, and our faith by our works (2 Pet. 1: 1–2).
We have become partakers of the divine nature (4). We
must add to our faith virtue, and then more knowledge,
self-control, perseverance, godliness, brotherly love and
love to all men (5–7). Only then will our knowledge
of Christ be productive (8). Only then shall we show
that we have not forgotten our first cleansing from sin

(9). Only then will our election be obvious (10). Only then shall we receive a rich entry into Christ's eternal Kingdom (11).

(b) *Love* or *Peace*. God's Kingdom is peaceful as well as righteous (cf. Isaiah 9: 6–7). So we must live in brotherly love now, not only 'without spot or blemish' but 'at peace' (2 Pet. 3: 14). Through the new birth, we are not only children of God (1 Pet. 1: 14) and heirs of the Kingdom (3–4), but brothers one of another (22–3). Therefore we must 'put away all malice and all guile and insincerity and envy and all slander' (1 Pet. 2: 1). Since 'the end of all things is at hand' we must 'above all hold unfailing our love for one another', practising hospitality and using our gifts for the common good (1 Pet. 4: 7–11). We must 'greet one another with the kiss of love' and wish 'peace to all . . . that are in Christ' (1 Pet. 5: 14).

(c) *Truth*. In heaven we shall 'know even as we are known' (1 Cor. 13: 9–12). Jesus Christ will be 'unveiled' and we shall see Him face to face (cf. 1 Pet. 1: 7–8). Meanwhile, we must grow in our knowledge of Him (2 Pet. 3: 18) and beware of false teachers (17). Peter devotes a large section of his second epistle (2 Pet. 1: 12–2: 22) to warning his readers against error. He repeats much of what Jude has already written in his epistle. He writes with words of strong indignation of the deceivers' brazen wickedness and fearful destiny (2 Pet. 2). He also indicates how his readers may continue in the truth after he is dead (2 Pet. 1: 13–14). They will still have two sources of authoritative teaching, the written apostolic word (15) which was based not on myths which they had invented but on history which they had witnessed (16–18), and the written prophetic word (19–21). The apostles of the New Testament were only confirming the prophets of the Old. Men 'spoke from God' (i.e., on His authority), not on their own impulse, but as they were irresistibly carried along by the inspiring Spirit (21). Let them therefore not be 'carried away with the error of lawless men and lose their own stability' (2 Pet. 3: 17) but keep growing in both the grace and the knowledge of their Lord and Saviour Jesus Christ (2 Pet. 3: 18).

Thus the Christian is to live this life in the light of the next and, like his Master before him, to enter into glory only through the fires of suffering. Simon Peter had learned this as 'a witness of the sufferings of Christ' (1 Pet. 5: 1) and of His glorious majesty (2 Pet. 1: 16). He had experienced its truth in his own case through the opposition of the Sanhedrin, and he is now led by the Holy Spirit to teach others what he has learned. No better conclusion could be found than the triumphant declaration with which he ends the argument of his first epistle (5: 10): 'After you have suffered a little while, the God of all grace, who has called you to His eternal glory in Christ, will Himself restore, establish and strengthen you. To Him be the dominion for ever and ever. Amen.'

Chapter VIII

THE MESSAGE OF THE REVELATION

. . . Jesus Christ the faithful witness, the firstborn of the dead, and the ruler of the kings on earth . . . Behold, He is coming with the clouds, and every eye will see Him.—Revelation 1: 5, 7

After this I looked, and lo, in heaven . . . an open door! . . . and lo, a throne stood in heaven, with one seated on the throne!—Revelation 4: 1, 2

IT is fitting that the Revelation should have been placed last in our New Testament. The historical situation of the Asian churches to which John was writing appears to belong to the close of the first century A.D. Persecution is no longer spasmodic and local, but systematic and widespread. The Church and the world are no longer skirmishing, but engaged in deadly combat. Nevertheless, there is no trace of fear or defeatism in the Revelation. 'The whole book is a *Sursum Corda*'.[1] John directs our gaze up to the eternal throne of the God who reigns over the affairs of men and nations, and on to the return of Him who will finally rout His enemies and rescue His Church.

But who is this 'John'? He describes himself by his simple, unadorned Christian name (1: 1, 4, 9; 22: 8). He is neither 'apostle' nor 'elder' nor even 'disciple'. He admits he is a 'prophet' (22: 9), but is content to call himself his readers' 'brother' and 'companion in the

[1] *The Apocalypse of St. John*, by H. B. Swete. (Macmillan, 1906.) p. xcii.

tribulation and the Kingdom and the endurance' which are 'in Jesus' (1: 9). He is writing from an involuntary exile on the island of Patmos in the Ægean Sea, where he has been sent on account of his preaching and his testimony to Jesus (1: 9). His book, which is strictly neither an epistle nor an apocalypse nor a prophecy, but a pastoral exhortation, is addressed to the seven principal churches in the Roman province of Asia (1: 11), and it is clear that he both knows their local conditions (geographical and spiritual), and that he can write to them with an authority which they will recognize. Further, his literary style, with its Semitic idioms and its astonishing barbarisms, betrays him as one who wrote in Greek but thought in Hebrew or Aramaic.

These are the principal facts which can be deduced from the internal evidence of the book itself. At first sight they accord satisfactorily with the traditional ascription of the book to St. John the apostle of Jesus and son of Zebedee. Justin Martyr is the first of the fathers to have thus clearly identified the author, and he belongs to the middle of the second century A.D. It was thereafter generally assumed that the apostle John was the author. At least as early as the middle of the third century, however, acceptance of the apostolic authorship of the Revelation was by no means universal. Dionysius, pupil of Origen and Bishop of Alexandria (A.D.247–65), drew attention to the striking divergence of both thought and language which is apparent between the Gospel and the Revelation. His opinion was that the author was another, but unknown, John. This led Eusebius, who reported Dionysius' view, to quote Papias' reference to John 'the elder' and to hazard the guess that this second John of Ephesus was the author of the Revelation. Many modern scholars have adopted his suggestion. But as many of them want this enigmatic presbyter as the author of the Gospel also, they are left with the original problem of how to believe that two such different works could have come from the pen of the same writer. Various other solutions have been attempted. The book has been called 'pseudonymous', as many of the contemporary Jewish apocalypses were, but this is 'scarcely possible'[1] since the supposed author assumes such an ambiguous name. Others have maintained that the book came from the same 'school', if not the same author, as the Gospel; or reveals traces of the work of compilers and subsequent editors; or is, as Dionysius wrote years ago, the product of an unknown John.

When all these alternative theories have been propounded and considered, we are left with the impression that the book is a unity; that it carried an earnest personal message to clearly defined Asian churches; that it was written by someone who knew them intimately, whose authority they respected and who can hardly have remained unknown; and that it can therefore only have come from such a well-known figure as John the elder (if he existed) or John the apostle. The differences of thought and style between the Gospel and the Revelation can be exaggerated. They are there, but there are also resemblances both in grammar and in vocabulary (e.g., 'witness', 'overcame', 'glory', 'hunger', 'thirst', 'life', 'Jew', 'sign', 'keep His words', 'true'). The inferior Greek may be due to dictation or translation. The discrepancy of thought can best be explained by a 'difference in the scope of the books'.[2] One is a 'gospel', the other an 'apocalypse'. The want of any satisfactory

---

[1] Swete, op. cit., p. clxx.
[2] Westcott, op. cit., p. lxxxvi.

alternative leads Swete 'to keep an open mind upon the question', but to 'incline to the traditional view' (p. 181).

More important than the exact identification of the author is an investigation of his fitness to convey his own particular theme. One of the strongest impressions gained from reading his book is his remarkable familiarity with the Old Testament Scriptures. He quotes from the law of Moses, the history books, the wisdom literature and the prophets. He is most at home in the Psalms and the prophets, and among the prophets he has a predilection for Isaiah, Ezekiel, Daniel and Zechariah. But his is no slavish recitation of former oracles. Indeed, he never deliberately quotes from any of them, and never draws the attention of his readers to the Scripture to which he is referring. He is so well versed in the Old Testament, that it is natural for him to employ, accurately yet freely, Old Testament language and imagery. More important still, he has assimilated the outlook of the Old Testament writers. He is acquainted with the history of God's ancient people. He knows that they had been slaves in Egypt, nomads in the desert, vassals of the empires of the east, exiles in Babylon and martyrs to the Greeks. But over and above the vicissitudes of their long history, he has heard the triumphant refrain 'The Lord reigneth'. He has not missed what Moses taught the fugitive Israelites, or Isaiah the hard-pressed Kingdom of Judah, or Ezekiel and Daniel the dispirited Babylonian exiles. He has imbibed the spirit of the Psalms and the faith of the prophets. It is probable that he also knew some of the contemporary Jewish apocalypses although the dating of some of them is disputed, and in them too, although their dating is uncertain and they do not belong to the sacred Scriptures, the triumph of God over evil is

L

confidently anticipated. What is quite clear is that man's invincible faith in the sovereignty of God had not died with the canon of the Old Testament. John shared it.

This introduces the second important fact about the author of the Revelation. It is that he had first-hand knowledge and personal experience of the world's hostility to Christ. The persecution which had broken out in the province of Asia seems to have been due largely to the Christians' refusal to be implicated in the worship of the Emperor. The cult of the Cæsars had been steadily growing. Julius Cæsar had been declared divine in 29 B.C., and there was a temple in his honour in Ephesus. Temples were erected to Augustus while he was still alive, and Tiberius followed suit. Caligula, the madman, with a passion for the praise of men, even attempted to defile the Holy of Holies in Jerusalem with an image of himself. Nero discouraged the cult, because he feared the death it seemed to herald, but Domitian outstripped all his predecessors in his thirst for the worship of his subjects. He liked his proconsuls to issue his orders under the title '*Dominus et Deus Noster*'. The province of Asia was particularly loyal. Every large Asian city had its 'Augusteum', or temple, dedicated to the Emperor. Only the Christians stood aside. Their creed was 'Jesus is Lord' (1 Cor. 12: 3). Nothing could induce them to sprinkle incense on the fire which burned before the Emperor's statue and say 'Cæsar is Lord'. Besides, many of the local festivals held in connexion with the imperial cult were associated with degrading idolatry and foul immorality. The Nicolaitans (2: 6, 15; cf. 2: 20) seem to have counselled the Christians to compromise. Had John in his earlier preaching urged his flock to renounce all contact with these hideous pagan practices? Had he reminded them that God is one and will not share His glory with another? Had he borne faithful witness to Jesus Christ as the only Lord to whom man's worship was due? Was this 'the word of God and the testimony of Jesus' (1: 9) for which he had been banished? His knowledge of the sore trials which the Asian churches were enduring, and his own experience of persecution will no doubt have brought to life the Old Testament message of God's eternal sovereignty.

Thirdly, John had a vision of the risen, glorified Jesus. It was the Lord's Day. The inspiring Spirit laid hold of him (1: 10). A loud voice told him to write what he saw and send it to the seven churches of Asia (1: 11). He turned and saw in the midst of seven golden lampstands 'one like a son of man' (1: 12-13). That is, he saw the man Christ Jesus. He was wearing His humanity still, but it was transfigured with glory. His robes were royal and priestly. His hair, like the Ancient of Days, was as white as snow. His eyes flashed like fire, His feet were strong as burnished bronze, and His voice sounded like the raging of the sea. He was holding in His right hand seven stars, which were 'the angels of the seven churches', and from His mouth issued a sharp two-edged sword, His piercing word. His face shone like the sun (1: 13-16), and John 'fell at His feet as though dead'(1: 17). It was this overwhelming vision of the Son of God which fitted John to write his book. Moses had seen God in the burning bush and 'hid his face, for he was afraid to look upon God' (Ex. 3: 6). Isaiah saw Him seated upon His throne high and lifted up, and the vision of His kingly majesty coloured his whole message (Is. 6). Ezekiel saw His glory on 'the likeness of a throne' (Ezek. 1). Daniel saw Him on the banks of the Tigris (Dan. 10: 2-9), and many features of the vision are recalled by that of John's. These men lived in days of crisis for their nation. God revealed to them His kingliness and His holiness, in order to inspire them, and through them the people, with repentance and faith. So it was with John. The infant Church was confronted by the vast might of the Roman Empire. It was a time of crisis. God's people were tempted to sin, to apostasy and to fear. John knew the vision which in older days had inspired the faithful to endure, but now he had seen it for himself. He had seen Jesus, risen, triumphant, glorious, invincible, holding the churches safely in His strong right hand. This was the vision needed by the persecuted Church.

John describes the character of his book in its very first verse, and in so doing gives us some important principles for its interpretation. It is an 'apocalypse', that is a 'revelation', or unveiling. First, he declares the *origin* of the revelation. It is a 'revelation . . . which God gave . . .'. True, it was designed for 'His servants' and was mediated to them through Christ and an angel and John, but it had a divine origin. John consciously and deliberately lays claim to this. His book is a 'prophecy' (1: 3; 22: 7, 10, 18), ranking in authority with Old Testament prophecies. He received it when he was 'in the Spirit' (1: 10; 4: 2; cf. 2: 7, etc.). He was commanded to record and dispatch what he saw (1: 11, 19; 22: 10). A special warning is given to those who tamper with the prophecy by adding to it or taking away from it (22: 18–19), and a special blessing is promised both to him who reads it aloud to the congregation and to them who hear and obey it (1: 3). This claim to divine origin is to be accepted. No interpretation of the book can be considered which fails to do it justice. It may not be dismissed as the strange vagaries of a fevered mind, or the mere human compilation of Jewish and early Christian apocalypses.

Secondly, John declares the *context* of the revelation. It is a revelation to the Church. God gave it 'to His servants'. Its destination was the people of God. Christ and the angel and the prophet are intermediaries. It is a message from God to His Church. John makes this clear in his first verse before going on in 1: 4 to write: 'John to the seven churches that are in Asia.' The Revelation had a genuine historical context. There were Christian churches in Ephesus and Smyrna, Pergamum and Thyatira, Sardis, Philadelphia and Laodicea (1: 11). John evidently exercised some kind of supervision over them, and to them he addressed his message. He even lists them in the order in which they would be reached by a messenger travelling along the great circular road which united them. This definite historical context is sufficient to dismiss the exaggerated 'futurist' school of interpretation which projects the fulfilment of the book's prophecies into the period immediately preceding the Lord's return. In this case, the book had no message for the churches for which John says he wrote it.

At the same time, beyond John's message to the local churches of first-century Asia is God's word to the universal Church of all generations. If this be so, the 'Præterist' school of interpretation must also be rejected. This sees in the events portrayed in the book not a prediction of the future but a description of the present. The book becomes a mere commentary on local, contemporary happenings and has little permanent value for the Church.

Thirdly, John describes the *character* of the revelation. It is a 'revelation of Jesus Christ'. This is the message required by a persecuted Church, whether it belongs to the first or the twentieth century. The historicist school of interpretation, which discoveres in the book a history of the world in code, tends to forget this essential principle. Quite apart from the multiplicity of interpretations which the historicists have suggested, modified, contradicted and withdrawn, the chief objection to this way of interpretation is that it loses sight of the Church's need. What a persecuted Church needs is not a detailed forecast of future events which has to be laboriously deciphered, but a vision of Jesus Christ to cheer the faint and encourage the weary. John's purpose is practical not academic. He is not just a seer but a pastor. His desire is not to satisfy our curiosity about the future but to stimulate our faithfulness in the present. He is told, it is true, 'what must soon take place', but all the future events which he foresees are presented in the light of Jesus Christ who is reigning now as 'ruler of the kings of the earth' (1: 5) and who is returning soon (1: 7). It is to Him that John directs his readers' attention, not just to the future. He is depicted in a variety of ways. We see Him among the lampstands, patrolling, investigating, encouraging the churches (1: 22–2: 1). Next, He is seen as the Lamb, close to the Father's throne, alone qualified to break the seals of the book of destiny (chs. 4–7). Then He is revealed as the Lord of the whole earth (11: 4, 8), delaying the final judgment until the Church's witness is completed. The scene changes again, and now He is the man-child to whom the sun-clothed woman gives birth and whom the dragon attempts to devour (12: 1–6). Soon He is portrayed as the warrior riding forth on a white horse at the head of the heavenly armies, to judge and make war against His enemies (19: 11–16). Finally, He is the Husband for whom the Church, His bride, descends from heaven adorned and perfected (21: 1–9).

This revelation of Christ is given in a series of visions. It is important to remember that they are self-contained visions. The visions are chronological, but the events represented in the visions need not be so. John saw one vision follow another. But it is not necessary to suppose that the visions reveal a historical sequence. They are successive visions of Christ. They are not visions of successive events. Many of the visions portray the same period, the Christian dispensation which stretches from the first to the second coming of Christ, but each has its different emphasis or insight. The book is not a film showing the continuous unfolding of one story but a series of lantern slides depicting the same landscape from different angles. Thus, the Seals, the Trumpets and the Bowls probably cover the same historical period, but with a different message. To give another example, in chapters 2 and 3 Christ is on earth 'walking among the lampstands' (2: 1), while in chapters 4 to 7 He is the Lamb 'as though it had been slain' who is in heaven close to the throne of God (5: 6). We are not to deduce from this that Christ first spent a period of fellowship with the churches on earth, and then spent another close to the throne of God in heaven. It is only the visions which succeeded one another in John's experience. Christ Himself is among the lampstands and near the throne at one and the same time. He is always present both with His Church on earth and with His Father in heaven.

Since they are visions, and moreover visions of Christ rather than of events, they have no exclusively particular historical reference. They reveal certain abiding, eternal principles governing Christ and His Church which are constantly illustrated in history. They certainly had an immediate fulfilment intelligible to the Asian churches (as the Præterists say); but they have been successively embodied in many other historical situations of later centuries (as the Historicists teach); they are apparent to-day; and they will receive a final and conclusive fulfilment at the end of the world (as the Futurists affirm). This 'successivist', 'parallelist' or 'continuous-historical' mode of interpretation preserves the essential emphasis in each of the other schools of exegesis.[1] The book then not only contains a well-defined message for the seven churches of Asia in the first century but also retains a message of permanent value for the Church of all places and of all ages. The historical situation has altered, but the spiritual principles remain.

The fourth hint which John gives in his first verse to help the reader to understand the book concerns the *method* of the revelation. It is a revelation in symbols. God 'signified' it through an angel to John. John employs the verb which is cognate to the favourite description in the fourth gospel of the miracles of Jesus as 'signs'. The visions of Jesus in the Revelation, like the works of Jesus in the Gospel, are spiritually significant. It is not the outward form which matters, but the inward meaning. The reasons for the use of 'signs' or symbolical visions in the Revelation are not hard to seek. They are not just intended to tax the ingenuity of succeeding generations of Christian believers! They were given partly to express heavenly truths which could not easily be put into words, and partly also to convey dangerous facts about the Empire which could not safely be written in direct speech.

The particular use of symbolism which is found in the Revelation concerns the imagery and the numbers. The imagery of the visions is very rich. It is derived

[1] See for this interpretation: *More Than Conquerors*, by W. Hendriksen (Tyndale Press, 1939).

from nature (e.g., horse, lamb, lion, locust, scorpion, eagle, tree, harvest, sea, rivers, earth, sky), from the life of man (e.g., commerce, warfare, childbirth, harlotry, agriculture, government, building), and from the Old Testament (e.g., Babylon, Jerusalem, Jezebel, Egypt, Sodom; the Temple and its furniture; manna; the tree and the book and the water of life; Jesus as Lamb, Lion, and Root, etc.). It is important to remember that much of the imagery, as in the parables which Jesus told, is added simply to give a heightened dramatic effect and does not possess an independent meaning in every detail. For instance, the gems enriching the walls of the Heavenly Jerusalem (21: 19) may not each symbolize something different. Further, the imagery is symbolical rather than pictorial, and is meant to be interpreted rather than visualized. We are not meant to imagine creatures 'full of eyes in front and behind' (4: 6), but to remember their ceaseless vigilance. We are not to conceive the white robes of the saints as having been literally laundered in a bath of the Lamb's blood, but to understand that their presence before the throne is due solely to the death of Jesus Christ (7: 9–14).

A clear symbolism also attaches to certain numbers, of which the most obvious are four, seven, and twelve, and multiples of them. Since there are four points of the compass and four winds of the earth, the number four appears to represent the created universe, and 'the four living creatures' worshipping round the throne seem to symbolize the dependence of the creation on its Creator. The number seven denotes completeness and perfection, probably because the creation story covers seven days in the book of Genesis. The seven churches of Asia, therefore, although historical, also represent the Catholic Church. Twelve is the number for the Church because

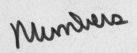

Numbers

there were twelve tribes in the Old Testament and twelve apostles in the New. The twenty-four elders seated round the throne must therefore symbolize the worshipping Church of both Testaments. The figure ten 'is suggestive at once of indefiniteness and of magnitude'[1] especially when another number is multiplied by it. Thus the 144,000 (7: 4; 14: 1), because it is 12 × 12 multiplied by 1,000, is an easily intelligible cipher for the redeemed Church, and similarly the millennium or the thousand years of 20: 4 is almost certainly to be interpreted not literally but symbolically of a very long but unspecified period. The only other number which should be mentioned now is the period defined indiscriminately as three and a half years (viz., 'a time, times and half a time'), 42 months and 1,260 days. If the month is reckoned as thirty days, this period is the same in each case. It appears to be the age of the New Covenant, the whole time elapsing between the first and second comings of Christ. It may be described as three and a half years because the whole of human history could be appropriately represented by the perfect 'seven years' and because Christ's coming divided it into two symbolically equal halves. The period of three and a half years is the age of the Church's persecution (cf. Dan. 7: 25 and 12: 7) and witness and nourishment by God (Rev. 11: 2, 3; 12: 6, 14; 13: 5).

Having defined his book as a revelation from God, for the Church, of Christ, in symbols, John proceeds to describe the series of visions given to him. The general theme is Christ and His Church, in conflict with many foes. It is perhaps best to divide the visions into six, and to give a rather compressed summary of them.

[1] Swete, op. cit. p. cxxxii.

(1) THE CHURCH'S LIFE IN CHRIST
(Chs. 1–3)

John first describes his vision of Christ's glory (1: 9–19) and then writes his letters which reveal the churches' condition (chs. 2–3). The sequence is important. The message to the churches issues from the vision of Christ. The message to each church contains three elements. First, it draws attention to some aspect of the glorified Christ taken from the vision or from His titles. Next, it lays emphasis upon one feature of the ideal Church. Thirdly, it promises some special reward to faithfulness. The key to this whole section is Christ 'among the lampstands' (1: 13; 2: 1). Walking in the midst of the churches is the Supreme Overseer. Christ is in the Church and the Church is in Christ. He can say to each congregation: 'I know your works', and so He can reveal to each its own condition, its Lord as it needs to see Him and its reward as will be most appropriate to each. Thus, the church in Ephesus has lost its first love (2: 1–7). The church in Smyrna is already enduring tribulation, but has more to suffer yet (2: 8–11). The church in Pergamum contains some who have compromised with evil, and needs to repent (2: 12–17). The church in Thyatira has much to commend it, but is rebuked for tolerating false teaching (2: 18–29). The church in Sardis lacks genuineness. It has a name for being alive, but is in reality dead (3: 1–6). The church in Philadelphia has an open door of evangelism to the surrounding provinces. Let it seize its special opportunities (3: 7–13). The church in Laodicea is lukewarm and self-satisfied, and lacks the humility to admit that it is poor and blind and naked (3: 14–22).

These then are the marks of the ideal Church—love,

suffering, holiness, sound doctrine, genuineness, evangelism and humility. They are what Christ desires to find in His churches as He walks among them.

(2) THE CHURCH'S SAFETY THROUGH CHRIST
(Chs. 4–7)

The scene changes. A new vision breaks. A door is opened in heaven. Christ is now revealed no longer 'like a son of man' (1: 13), among the lampstands, but like a lamb 'as though it had been slain' (5: 6), near God's throne. The same Lord Jesus who walks among His churches on earth presides over the destinies of His Church from heaven. The Church which derives its life from Christ owes its safety to Christ. Every feature of the vision emphasizes the security of the people of God. The three Persons of the Blessed Trinity are active in the preservation of the Church. First, John sees the throne, which the Father occupies. When the door is opened in heaven, John's eye lights immediately on a throne, the symbol of divine sovereignty. God reigns, surrounded by worshipping hosts—twenty-four elders (representing the Church), four living creatures (representing the creation) and myriad angels (chs. 4–5). Next, John sees the scroll which only the Son can open. The scroll is sealed on both sides with seven seals. It is the book of destiny. No one is worthy to break the seals except the slaughtered Lamb—the Saviour who still bears the marks of His passion (ch. 5). In his vision John sees the Lamb open the seals one by one, and as a result a series of catastrophes (6: 1–8) overtakes the world (military aggression, bloodshed, food shortage, and death), the martyrs are heard crying: 'O Sovereign Lord . . . how long . . .?' (6: 9–11) and finally, the day of judgment arrives (6: 12–17). But none of these misfortunes befalls the earth until the Lamb breaks a seal of the book, for they are subject to His permission. Then thirdly, John sees the seal which the Holy Spirit uses. He sees two companies, the first numbering a hundred and forty-four thousand—twelve thousand from each of the tribes of Israel (7: 1–8), and the second a countless multitude from every nation (7: 9–17). The first are all 'sealed . . . upon their foreheads' (7: 3). Indeed, the final calamity is delayed until the sealing is completed. The Holy Spirit is not mentioned by name, but other passages in the New Testament indicate that it is He who seals the believer (e.g., Eph. 1: 13–14). Several different explanations have been given of the two multitudes, that they are the Jewish and Christian Churches respectively, or the Hebrew-Christian and Gentile-Christian Churches. It is perhaps more probable that the same completed Church is intended in each case, but that in the first vision it is the Church militant on earth, marshalled in battle array like the twelve tribes in the wilderness, counted and sealed for security; whereas in the other vision it is the Church triumphant in heaven, countless, cosmopolitan and finally redeemed.

The general theme of these chapters is clear. Whatever trials may beset the Church, it is secure through the sovereignty of God.

(3) THE CHURCH'S WITNESS TO CHRIST
(Chs. 8–11)

When the seventh seal is opened, there is silence in heaven. No vision appears to complete the series, for the end is not yet. Instead, another series of visions begins, each introduced this time not by the opening of a seal but by the blowing of a trumpet. The calamities which result are similar to the previous ones, but more severe. It is suggested that the trumpets give the clue to their meaning. When an event occurs after the opening of a seal, it is to be viewed as permitted by Christ, but when it occurs after the blowing of a trumpet, it is to be viewed as a divine warning (cf. Ezek. 33: 3). The seals reassure the Church and beget faith. The trumpets warn the world and beget repentance. At least, that is their purpose (like the plagues in Egypt which they intentionally resemble), although it is written (9: 20) 'the rest of mankind . . . did not repent . . .'. There are seven warnings, the first four comparatively mild (8: 1–12) and the last three so serious as to be termed 'woes' (8: 13; 9: 12; 11: 14). Now this activity of God is accompanied by the activity of the Church. God's warnings and the Church's witness go hand in hand. Christ who is the source of the Church's life and the guarantee of the Church's safety is also the object of the Church's witness.

Before the final woe breaks upon the impenitent world (10: 1–7), John is given a scroll which he eats, to symbolize that he has digested its contents, and then he is told to prophesy again (10: 8–11). Nor is it only he who preaches. God gives His 'two witnesses power to prophesy' throughout the New Testament period, 'clothed in sackcloth' (11: 3). The two witnesses seem to represent the witnessing Church, 'two' perhaps to emphasize the Church's 'fellowship in the gospel' (Phil. 1: 5), as Jesus sent out the seventy, two by two (Lk. 10: 1), or to suggest the witness of the Old and New Testament Churches, or to ensure the effectiveness of a witness borne by two (Deut. 19: 15), and to recall Zechariah's prophecy (Zech. 4) referred to in 11: 4. The two witnesses warn the world, like the first six plagues, and when their testimony is finished they will be killed (11: 7), and for a short time there will be no Christian witness. Then the Church will revive after its persecution (11: 11) before its final translation to glory (11: 12–13) and the final judgment of the world (11: 14–19). The vision ends with God's temple opened in heaven and God dwelling among His people (11: 19). But this consummation will not take place until the number of the elect (7: 3) and the witness of the Church (11: 7) are alike completed.

(4) THE CHURCH'S CONFLICT FOR CHRIST
(Chs. 12–14)

The Book of the Revelation is clearly divided into two parts, and the break occurs between chapter 11 and chapter 12. Chapter 11 ends with the final judgment and with the beginning of heaven. It might have been the end of the book. But now the curtain is raised further. The door is opened wider. John's readers are taken behind the scenes. The secret issues are revealed. Superficially, the conflict is between the Church and the world. Two empires confront one another. One is the Kingdom of God or the Empire of Christ, but the other is not the Roman Empire. It is the Kingdom of Satan. The Lamb and the Dragon are the real combatants. So in chapters 12 to 14 we are introduced to the Church's enemies, the dragon (ch. 12) who is Satan, and his three allies—the beast from the sea (13: 1–10), the beast from the earth (13: 11–18) who is also called the false prophet (19: 20; 20: 10), and the scarlet woman (17) who is also called 'the great harl'ot (17: 1) and 'Babylon the great' (14: 8). 'The great red dragon' (12:

1) is identified as 'that ancient serpent, who is called the Devil and Satan, the deceiver of the whole world' (12: 9). He is introduced in three scenes. The first is his attempt on Christ (12: 1–6), who is the man-child born of the twelve-crowned woman clearly representing the Church. The second is his flight from heaven (12: 7–12). Christ by His death (Col. 2: 15; Heb. 2: 14) and exaltation has conquered the devil for ever. He has been cast out of heaven, although he continues to attack the Church on earth. The third is his pursuit of the Church (12: 13–17). Foiled in his attack on Christ (12: 1–5) and on the Church as a whole (12: 6, 13–16), he directs his attention to individual Christian believers (12: 17). In doing so, he summons his allies. The first is the Beast from the Sea. He is the Roman Empire. His seven heads are both the seven hills of Rome and seven Roman emperors (17: 9–11), and his ten horns are a large number (perhaps intentionally indefinite) of other kings who are later to bear rule and will cause the downfall of the Empire (17: 15–18). To this beast the dragon gives his great authority (13: 2), for the Roman Empire is viewed as a persecuting world-power. True, one of the beast's heads had received a mortal wound, but it was now healed (13: 3). That is, Nero, the first persecuting emperor was dead, but his policy had been revived by Domitian. 'The number of the beast is 666' (13: 18), and perhaps the most reasonable explanation of this cryptogram is as follows: the letters of the Hebrew alphabet all possess a numerical value and are used instead of numbers. Now if the words 'Nero Cæsar' are written in Hebrew, and if the letters are read as numbers and the numbers then added up, the total is 666. This beast, with its mystic number, is followed and worshipped by the whole earth (12: 3–4, 7, 8), blasphemes

against God (12: 5–6), and persecutes the Church (12: 7).

The chief characteristic of the second beast which arises out of the earth is that it causes the inhabitants of the earth to worship the first beast (13: 12). In doing so, it uses magical arts (13: 13–15) and boycotts those who will not do homage to the first beast (13: 16–18). If the first beast is the persecuting Empire, the second is the Cæsar-cult. The emperors were not content to persecute the Christians. They tried to persuade them to give them their worship.

Before introducing the dragon's third ally, John recounts another vision, whose purpose is to reassure the struggling Church. It depicts the Lamb on Mount Zion surrounded by His one hundred and forty-four thousand redeemed ones who have upon their foreheads not the name of the beast (13: 16–18) but His own name and His Father's (14: 1–5). Then follows an episode in which a series of angels is featured. The first calls the world to worship God and warns of the imminent judgment (14: 6–7). The second announces the fall of the dragon's third ally, who is now mentioned for the first time. 'Fallen, fallen is Babylon the great, she who made all nations drink the wine of her impure passion' (14: 8). This, too, is Rome, viewed now not as Persecutor or Idolator but as Tempter. She is 'the great harlot' who seduces the unwary and draws them away from allegiance to God. She sits on the first beast. She is 'arrayed in purple and scarlet, and bedecked with gold and jewels and pearls', and on her forehead is written: 'Babylon the great, mother of harlots and of earth's abominations' (17: 1–5). The harlot is Rome's vice and moral licence, her corrupting and demoralizing influence. She is 'the pomp and vanity of this wicked world'.

M

These, then, are the dragon's allies. They have re-
appeared throughout the history of the world. The beast
emerges from the sea whenever antichristian authority
persecutes the Church. The beast from the earth is
reincarnate in every antichristian philosophy which
deceives the Church. The scarlet woman flaunts her vile
charms wherever antichristian morality contaminates
the Church. Through restrictive legislation and heresy
and worldliness the devil still pursues and seeks to
destroy the Church of Jesus Christ.

(5) THE CHURCH'S VINDICATION BY CHRIST
(Chs. 15–20)

Already the judgment of the devil and his allies has
been announced. Another angel has warned those who
will worship the beast that judgment will consume them
(14: 9–11), and has urged the saints to endure (14: 12).
Already we catch a glimpse of the Heavenly Reaper
with a crown on His head and a sickle in His hand, and
we known that the dreadful time of harvesting is near
(14: 14–20). These episodes prepare for the seven bowls
of wrath in chapter 16, which give a panorama of the
final overthrow of evil in its many forms and are themselves introduced by a prologue (ch. 15) in which the
redeemed saints sing 'the song of Moses . . . and of the
Lamb' (15: 3) which is a grand justification of the ways
of God in judgment. Then the seven bowls of wrath
are poured out. The eye of faith which sees in the opening of the seals the permissive will of God and in the
blowing of the trumpets the reformative purpose of
God, sees in the pouring out of the bowls the retributive
justice of God. The bowls introduce events which are
final and irrevocable. Next, the three allies of the dragon

are dismissed in the opposite order to that in which they were introduced. Babylon, the great harlot, is elaborately described (17: 1–6), then interpreted (17: 7–18) and finally overthrown (18: 1–19: 10). The old funeral dirge which Isaiah sang at the first Babylon's overthrow (Is. 13) is sung again at the fall of Rome and of all ungodly empires. Kings (18: 9–10) and merchants (18: 11–20) and angels (18: 2–3, 21–4) hail her downfall, and the great heavenly multitude (19: 1–10) shouts its 'Hallelujah', because the judgment of the harlot is just (19: 2) and the marriage of the Lamb has come (19: 7).

The next visions describe the overthrow of the beasts (19: 11–21). Christ, Judge and Word of God and King, rides forth on a white horse to smite the nations (19: 11–16). The birds flying in mid-heaven are summoned to gather for 'the great supper of God' (19: 17–18), and the armies of the earth gather for the final conflict. The beasts are captured and cast into the lake of fire (19: 19–21). The final vision in this series depicts the overthrow of the dragon himself. If the vision recapitulates, like the others, the whole of the Christian dispensation, then the binding of Satan for a thousand years refers to this same period. Certainly 'the strong man armed' was 'bound' (cf. Mk. 3: 27) when Christ first came, and the saints shared in His resurrection and reign (Eph. 2: 4–6). Before the end, however, Satan will be 'loosed for a little while' (20 :3), will gather the nations together for the last battle, called the Battle of Armageddon (19: 17–21; 20: 7–10), and will be thrown into the lake of fire where the two beasts are (20: 7–10). Then the judgment of the great white throne will take place, and all the dead, small and great, will stand before the throne and those whose names are not 'found written in the book of life' will be 'thrown into the lake of fire' (20: 11–15).

(6) THE CHURCH'S UNION WITH CHRIST
(Chs. 21–2)

Having witnessed the final judgment of the world (chs. 15–20), John now sees the final destiny of the Church (chs. 21–2). The one is complementary to the other. The overthrow of the world is accompanied by the triumph of the Church. The union of the Church with Christ in heaven is purely spiritual, but it is portrayed under material symbols. The new heaven and the new earth (21: 2) are described in terms strongly reminiscent of Old Testament phraseology. Indeed, the Old Testament prophetic anticipations will be perfectly fulfilled in the glorified Church. John sees first an adorned bride (21: 1–8). The harlot Babylon is no more. The bride of Christ remains. God has betrothed His Israel to Him for ever. Next John sees a walled city (21: 9–27). The great city is no more. The holy city remains. Babylon has fallen. Jerusalem abides. It has 'the glory of God' (21: 11, 23). That is, it enjoys the manifested presence of God. There is 'no temple in the city, for its temple is the Lord God the Almighty and the Lamb' (21: 22). The whole city is the Holy of Holies. Thirdly, John sees a watered garden (22: 1–5). The Garden of Eden appears again, with its tree of life. Paradise Lost is Paradise Regained.

Each of these three visions finally fulfils what has been predicted in the Old Testament and partially fulfilled through the gospel. We are already the pure bride of Christ (2 Cor. 11: 2). We have already come unto Mount Zion (Heb. 12: 22). We have already begun to drink of the water of life (John 4 and 7: 37–9). But the

consummation will far exceed the Church's present experience. God already dwells in His Church as in His
temple (1 Cor. 3: 16; Eph. 2: 19–22), but then our
fellowship with Him through Christ will be perfect.
This assurance accompanies each of the three visions.
'Behold, the dwelling of God is with men' (21: 3). 'Its
temple is the Lord God the Almighty and the Lamb'
(21: 22). 'The river of the water of life' flows 'from the
throne of God and of the Lamb' (22: 1). 'His servants
shall worship Him; they shall see His face; and His name
shall be on their foreheads' (22: 3, 4).

The book ends with solemn warnings. The reader
must neither disobey it (22: 6–9), nor seal it (22: 10–17),
nor tamper with it (22: 18–21). The reason in each case
is: 'I am coming soon' (22: 7, 12, 20). The phrase brings
us back to the place where we began (1: 1). We are to
live our lives in the light of Christ—of His present reign
and of His future return.

The book is finished. Across the screen of the seer's
receptive mind the Holy Spirit has flashed symbolical
picture-visions of the Church's unavoidable conflicts,
assured safety and ultimate triumph. Above and beyond
them all is Jesus Christ Himself, walking among the
lampstands as the Son of man (1: 13–2: 1), standing
before the Throne as the Lamb-Lion (5: 5–6), and
riding upon a white horse as the King of Kings (19:
11–13). This is, in brief, the grand theme of the book.
For its inner life a sinful Church needs the vision of
Christ residing in it. For its outer conflict a doubtful
Church needs the vision of Christ reigning over it. For
its ultimate destiny a fearful Church needs the vision of
Christ returning to it. To a sinful Church the residing
Christ says: 'I know. . . . Repent!' To a doubtful Church
the reigning Christ says: 'I have conquered . . . .

Believe!' To a fearful Church Christ says: 'I am coming soon. . . . Endure.' This is Christ's word to the Church of all ages. So the Bride responds, as the Spirit does, with words of joyful expectation: 'Even so, come, Lord Jesus' (22: 17, 20).

CONCLUSION

DESIRING to grasp the meaning of the New Testament, it has been necessary to isolate each writer's particular theme. To do this is helpful, but it can be very misleading. It is not intended to suggest that the apostolic writers were contradicting or correcting one another. The difference between them is one of emphasis only, and their themes blend harmoniously into one balanced symphony. Even the casual reader cannot fail to be impressed by their remarkable unanimity. They are *men with a message*. The men were many; but the message is one. The Holy Spirit chose and fashioned each author, fitting him to convey his distinctive theme, but when their contributions are added together in the canon of the New Testament, the message forms one coherent whole. Indeed, this is to be expected, for behind the human thoughts is the one divine Mind, and behind the human writers is the one divine Author. The Holy Spirit 'who spake by the prophets' spake by the apostles also. Jesus Himself had promised that it would be so, when He said: 'I have yet many things to say to you, but you cannot bear them now. When the Spirit of truth comes, He will guide you into all the truth; for He will not speak on His own authority, but whatever He hears He will speak, and He will declare to you the things that are to come. He will glorify Me, for He will take what is Mine and declare it to you' (John 16: 12–14). Having now examined separately each message, and the man who conveyed it, it will be wise to step back and survey the whole.

The message is first and foremost a declaration. It is good news about God. It is the story of what God has done in and through His Son Jesus Christ, our Lord and Saviour. He has established His Kingdom. True, the full manifestation of the Kingdom is yet to come. We await the final consummation. But the Kingdom of God has been inaugurated. The time has been fulfilled. The dreams of ancient visionaries have come true. God has kept His promise to Abraham. Long centuries of Old Testament expectation have at last materialized. The new age has dawned. The New Covenant has been ratified through the bloodshedding of Jesus. Those who repent of their sins, renounce themselves and believe in Christ hear the covenant promise '. . . I will be their God, and they shall be My people . . . for I will forgive their iniquity, and I will remember their sin no more' (Jer. 31: 33–4).

This good news is for everyone. Doctor Luke, Gentile historian and traveller, lays his emphasis on the universality of the gospel. No one is beyond its embrace. Men and women, children and adults, rich and poor, Jews and Gentiles, the outcasts and the righteous —all may come, for 'all flesh shall see the salvation of God'.

It is given to Paul to expound why this is so. He had been narrowly Judaistic in outlook, and had been seeking to earn God's favour through his own good works done in obedience to the law. He came to see that salvation is a gift which is offered freely to all men on account of Christ's atoning sacrifice on the cross. It is universal because it is free. There are no privileges now. The great condition is faith. 'The gospel of Christ . . . is the power of God unto salvation to everyone who believes . . .' (Rom. 1: 16). Faith is the open, empty hand which receives God's gift. The work is God's. It is by His grace that we are what we are. It is by grace that we are justified, and the grace which justifies is the grace which sanctifies and edifies and will finally glorify. It is all 'by grace through faith' (Eph. 2: 8).

This offer of God in the gospel is not only universal and free. It is also final. The covenant which God has established with men through Christ's unique sacrifice and perpetual priesthood is an everlasting covenant. The new covenant is the last covenant. It is not just another stage in the unfolding of God's purposes. It will never pass away. It is the grand finale on earth, concluding many acts and many scenes. The writer to the Hebrews, steeped as he is in the Old Testament anticipation, is well qualified to demonstrate Christ's superiority to all that has gone before.

Free and final as the New Covenant is, it must not be thought that its beneficiaries may enjoy their privileges with idle and sinful irresponsibility. Paul has said this many times. The writer to the Hebrews has urged his readers, in view of the finality of the Christian religion, to hold fast and to grow in faith, hope and love. But James the Just, zealous for the law, is entrusted more than others with the message of good works. Let there be no mistake. True religion is a matter of deeds not words, of practice not profession, of behaviour not just belief. A man with real faith will manifest his faith by his works. True religion is practical, not theoretical. It will show itself in obedience to God, in self control and in love. Saving faith is a faith which works.

But Christianity is not just living a good life. Christianity is the enjoyment of eternal life. It is life abundant, which is the personal knowledge of God (Jn. 17: 3) and which begins here and now because it is in Christ (Jn. 1: 3). So John, the beloved disciple, bears witness to Jesus, his beloved Master. His gospel is designed to set forth Jesus Christ. He desires his readers to see the divine glory of Jesus in His words and works, to believe in Him and so to receive life (Jn. 20:31). Not content with this, he wishes his 'little children' who possess eternal life to know it (1 Jn. 5: 12–13), and he reminds them of the truth and the obedience and the love which alone can prove that they are born of God.

The wonder of this eternal life is manifest. The believer who has entered into it is privileged indeed. Nevertheless, he has much to suffer. Simon Peter learned this through bitter experience. His Lord had had to suffer in order to enter into His glory. Peter had had to suffer, too. So also the Christians in Asia Minor would not escape 'the sufferings of the Christ'. They must be patient as He was, knowing that they would be partakers of the glory which was to be revealed.

That glory John unfolds more elaborately in the Book of the Revelation. He knows the enemies of Christ and His Church, their power and their cunning. Exiled himself, and in touch with the persecuted Asian churches, he knows the fury of the dragon, the authority of the beast, the deceit of the false prophet and the bewitching charms of the harlot Babylon. But he has also seen Christ glorified. A door has been opened in heaven. He has seen a throne, and One who sat on the throne. The Christians must hold fast. God reigns, and Christ will return in glory. Evil will be eradicated. The dragon and his allies will be cast into the lake of fire together with everyone whose name is not found written in the Lamb's book of life. And then God will make all things new. The new heaven and the new earth will appear, for the first heaven and the first earth will pass away (Rev. 22: 1). The final state will bring to perfection all prophetic expectations and abundantly satisfy all human desires. The New Jerusalem, resplendent with jewels, will descend from heaven. Through the middle of the street of the city, issuing from the throne of God and of the Lamb, will flow the river of the water of life, bright as crystal (Rev. 22: 1). He who is thirsty may come. He who desires may take of the water of life without price (Rev. 22: 17). So shall the New Covenant have been consummated, and a great voice from the throne shall say: 'Behold, the dwelling of God is with men. He will dwell with them, and they shall be His people, and God Himself will be with them; He will wipe away every tear from their eyes, and death shall be no more, neither shall there be mourning nor crying nor pain any more, for the former things have passed away.'[1]

Then at last, God will be 'everything to everyone'.[2]

---

[1] Rev. 21: 3-4.
[2] 1 Cor. 15: 28.